NAVNEET'S

LOGARITHMIC AND MATHEMATICAL TABLES

(WITH USEFUL DATA)

For Schools and Colleges

❄ INDEX ❄

NAVNEET®

NAVNEET EDUCATION LIMITED

Navneet Bhavan, Bhavani Shankar Road, Dadar, **Mumbai – 400 028.** (Tel. 6662 6565)

Navneet House, Gurukul Road, Memnagar, **Ahmadabad – 380 052.** (Tel. 6630 5000)

www.navneet.com ● **e-mail :** publications@navneet.com

A 0101

1. SOME CONVERSION FACTORS

1. Mass and Density :

1 kg = 1000 g

1 u = 1.661×10^{-27} kg

1 kg/m^3 = 10^{-3} g/cm^3

2. Length, Area and Volume :

1 m = 100 cm = 39.37 in
= 3.281 ft

1 mi = 1.609 km = 5280 ft

1 in = 2.54 cm

1 nm = 10^{-9} m = 10 Å

1 pm = 10^{-12} m = 1000 fm

1 Å = 10^{-8} cm = 10^{-10} m = 0.1 nm
= 100 pm

1 light year = 9.46×10^{15} m

1 m^2 = 10^4 cm^2

1 mL = 1 cm^3 = 10^{-3} L = 10^{-3} dm^3
= 10^{-6} m^3

1 m^3 = 10^3 dm^3 = 10^3 L = 10^6 mL
= 10^6 cm^3

1 L = 10^3 mL = 10^3 cm^3 = 1 dm^3
= 10^{-3} m^3

3. Time :

1 d = 86400 s

1 y = $365\frac{1}{4}$ d = 3.16×10^7 s

4. Angular Measure :

1 rad = $\frac{180°}{\pi}$ = 57.3° (plane angle)

π rad = 180° = $\frac{1}{2}$ rev (plane angle)

5. Speed :

1 m/s = 3.28 ft/s = 2.24 mi/h

1 km/h = 0.621 mi/h = 0.278 m/s

6. Force and Pressure :

1 N = 10^5 dynes = 0.225 lb

1 ton = 1000 kg

1 Pa = 1 N/m^2 = 10 dyn/cm^2

1 atm = 1.013×10^5 Pa
= 1.013×10^5 N/m^2
= 76 cm Hg

7. Energy and Power :

1 J = 10^7 ergs = 0.2389 cal

1 kW·h = 3.6×10^6 J

1 cal = 4.186 J

1 eV = 1.602×10^{-19} J

8. Magnetism :

1 T = 1 Wb/m^2 = 10^4 gauss

MISCELLANEOUS

$\pi = 3.1416$, $\pi^2 = 9.87$, $\frac{1}{\pi} = 0.3183$

$e = 2.718$, $\log_{10} e = 0.4343$, $\log_e 10 = 2.303$, $\log_e x = 2.303 \log_{10} x$

Gravitational constant, $G = 6.673 \times 10^{-11}$ N·m^2/kg^2

Universal gas constant, $R = 8.315$ J/mol·K

Avogadro constant, $N_A = 6.022 \times 10^{23}$ mol^{-1}

Boltzmann constant, $k = 1.381 \times 10^{-23}$ J/K

Stefan-Boltzmann constant, $\sigma = 5.670 \times 10^{-8}$ W/m^2·K^4

Speed of light in free space, $c = 2.998 \times 10^8$ m/s

Elementary charge, $e = 1.602 \times 10^{-19}$ C

Permittivity constant, $\varepsilon_0 = 8.854 \times 10^{-12}$ F/m

Permeability constant, $\mu_0 = 1.257 \times 10^{-6}$ H/m

Planck constant, $h = 6.626 \times 10^{-34}$ J·s

Rydberg constant, $R = 1.097 \times 10^7$ m^{-1}

Electron mass, $m_e = 9.109 \times 10^{-31}$ kg

Proton mass, $m_p = 1.673 \times 10^{-27}$ kg

Neutron mass, $m_n = 1.675 \times 10^{-27}$ kg

2. ALGEBRA

* $\log_a x = y \Leftrightarrow x = a^y$, $a > 0$, $a \neq 1$, $x > 0$.

  $\log_q p = \log_q r \cdot \log_r p$

* Sum of first n terms of an A.P. with first term a and common difference d is $\frac{1}{2} n[2a+(n-1)d] = n \times$ (average of first and last terms).

* Sum of first n terms of a G.P. with first term a and common ratio r is $\frac{a(1-r^n)}{1-r} = \frac{a(r^n-1)}{r-1}$, $(r \neq 1)$

* $\sum_{r=1}^{n} r = \frac{n}{2}(n+1)$; $\quad \sum_{r=1}^{n} r^2 = \frac{n}{6}(n+1)(2n+1)$;

  $\sum_{r=1}^{n} r^3 = \frac{n^2}{4}(n+1)^2$

* If $f(x) \equiv ax^2 + bx + c$, where $a \neq 0$, $a, b, c \in R$, then roots α, β of $f(x) = 0$ are given by $\frac{-b \pm \sqrt{b^2 - 4ac}}{2a}$. Also, $\alpha + \beta = \frac{-b}{a}$, $\alpha\beta = \frac{c}{a}$.

  Roots will be real if $b^2 - 4ac \geqslant 0$ and imaginary if $b^2 - 4ac < 0$.

* Remainder when polynomial $P(x)$ is divided by $(x - a)$ is $P(a)$

* Number of combinations of n objects taken r at a time

  ^nC_r or $\binom{n}{r} = \frac{n!}{(n-r)!r!}$, where $n! = n(n-1)(n-2) \ldots 3 \cdot 2 \cdot 1$

  Binomial Theorem :

  $(1 \pm x)^n = {^nC_0} \pm {^nC_1}\, x + {^nC_2}\, x^2 \pm \ldots\ldots + (-1)^r\, {^nC_r} x^r + \ldots\ldots + (-1)^n x^n$,

  where $^nC_r = \frac{n!}{r!(n-r)!}$.

3. COORDINATE GEOMETRY

(1) **Distance formula :**

$d = \sqrt{(x_2 - x_1)^2 + (y_2 - y_1)^2}$, where d is the distance between two points having coordinates (x_1, y_1) and (x_2, y_2).

(2) **Section formulae :**

The coordinates of the point which divides the join of (x_1, y_1) and (x_2, y_2)

(i) *internally* in the ratio $m : n$ are $\left(\frac{mx_2 + nx_1}{m+n}, \frac{my_2 + ny_1}{m+n}\right)$

(ii) *externally* in the ratio $m : n$ are $\left(\frac{mx_2 - nx_1}{m-n}, \frac{my_2 - ny_1}{m-n}\right)$

(iii) in two equal parts (i.e. midpoint) are $\left(\frac{x_1 + x_2}{2}, \frac{y_1 + y_2}{2}\right)$

(3) Centroid of the Δ ABC, where coordinates of A, B, C are

$(x_1, y_1), (x_2, y_2), (x_3, y_3)$ has coordinates $\left(\frac{x_1+x_2+x_3}{3}, \frac{y_1+y_2+y_3}{3}\right)$

(4) Slope of the line containing the segment with end points $(x_1, y_1), (x_2, y_2)$ is given by :

$$m = \frac{y_2-y_1}{x_2-x_1} = \frac{\text{Difference of ordinates}}{\text{Difference of abscissae}}, \text{ where } (x_2-x_1) \neq 0$$

(5) Acute angle α between two lines with slopes m_1 and m_2 is given by

$$\tan \alpha = \left|\frac{m_1-m_2}{1+m_1 m_2}\right|, \text{ where } m_1 m_2 \neq -1$$

Two lines with slopes m_1 and m_2 will be parallel if $m_1 = m_2$.

Two lines with slopes m_1 and m_2 will be perpendicular if $m_1 m_2 = -1$.

4. MENSURATION

Geometrical Form	Perimeter	Area	Volume
Rectangle (sides a, b)	$2a+2b$	ab	....
Square (side a)	$4a$	a^2	....
Triangle (base a, altitude h)	....	$\frac{1}{2}ah$	....
Triangle (sides a, b, c)	$a+b+c = 2s$	$\sqrt{s(s-a)(s-b)(s-c)}$, where $s = \frac{a+b+c}{2}$	....
Circle (radius r)	$2\pi r$	πr^2	....
Ellipse (axes $2a$, $2b$)	$2\pi\sqrt{\frac{a^2+b^2}{2}}$ app.	πab	....
Cylinder (radius r, height h)	....	$2\pi r(h+r)$	$\pi r^2 h$
Cone (radius r, height h, slant height l)	....	$\pi r(l+r)$	$\frac{1}{3}\pi r^2 h$
Sphere (radius r)	....	$4\pi r^2$	$\frac{4}{3}\pi r^3$
Anchor ring (mean radius R, radius of circular section r)	....	$4\pi^2 r R$	$2\pi^2 r^2 R$

5. TRIGONOMETRY

(a) $\frac{\sin\theta}{\cos\theta} = \tan\theta$

$\sin^2\theta + \cos^2\theta = 1$

$1 + \tan^2\theta = \sec^2\theta$

$1 + \cot^2\theta = \text{cosec}^2\theta$

$\sin(90° - \theta) = \cos\theta$

$\cos(90° - \theta) = \sin\theta$

$\sin(180° - \theta) = \sin\theta$

$\cos(180° - \theta) = -\cos\theta$

$\sin^2\theta = \frac{1-\cos 2\theta}{2}$

$\cos^2\theta = \frac{1+\cos 2\theta}{2}$

$\tan^2\theta = \frac{1-\cos 2\theta}{1+\cos 2\theta}$

$\sin(\theta \pm \phi) = \sin\theta \cdot \cos\phi \pm \cos\theta \cdot \sin\phi$

$\cos(\theta \pm \phi) = \cos\theta \cdot \cos\phi \mp \sin\theta \cdot \sin\phi$

$$\tan(\theta \pm \phi) = \frac{\tan\theta \pm \tan\phi}{1 \mp \tan\theta \cdot \tan\phi}$$

$$\sin 2\theta = 2 \sin \theta \cdot \cos \theta = \frac{2 \tan\theta}{1+\tan^2\theta}$$

$$\cos 2\theta = \cos^2\theta - \sin^2\theta = 2\cos^2\theta - 1 = 1 - 2\sin^2\theta = \frac{1-\tan^2\theta}{1+\tan^2\theta}$$

$$\sin 3\theta = 3\sin\theta - 4\sin^3\theta;\ \cos 3\theta = 4\cos^3\theta - 3\cos\theta$$

$$\sin A + \sin B = 2\sin\left(\frac{A+B}{2}\right)\cdot\cos\left(\frac{A-B}{2}\right)$$

$$\sin A - \sin B = 2\cos\left(\frac{A+B}{2}\right)\cdot\sin\left(\frac{A-B}{2}\right)$$

$$\cos A + \cos B = 2\cos\left(\frac{A+B}{2}\right)\cdot\cos\left(\frac{A-B}{2}\right)$$

$$\cos A - \cos B = -2\sin\left(\frac{A+B}{2}\right)\cdot\sin\left(\frac{A-B}{2}\right)$$

If $\tan\frac{x}{2} = t$, $\sin x = \frac{2t}{1+t^2}$, $\cos x = \frac{1-t^2}{1+t^2}$, $\tan x = \frac{2t}{1-t^2}$

(b) In any triangle :

(i) $\frac{a}{\sin A} = \frac{b}{\sin B} = \frac{c}{\sin C} = 2R$ **(sine rule),**

(ii) $a^2 = b^2 + c^2 - 2bc\cos A$ **(cosine rule),**

(iii) $\sin\frac{A}{2} = \sqrt{\frac{(s-b)(s-c)}{bc}}$, (iv) $\cos\frac{A}{2} = \sqrt{\frac{s(s-a)}{bc}}$,

(v) Radius of circumcircle, $R = \frac{abc}{4\Delta}$ (where Δ = area of triangle)

(vi) Radius of inscribed circle, $r = \frac{\Delta}{s}$ (where Δ = area of triangle)

Trigonometrical ratios of special angles

θ	0°	30°	45°	60°	90°
sin	0	$\frac{1}{2}$	$\frac{1}{\sqrt{2}}$	$\frac{\sqrt{3}}{2}$	1
cos	1	$\frac{\sqrt{3}}{2}$	$\frac{1}{\sqrt{2}}$	$\frac{1}{2}$	0
tan	0	$\frac{1}{\sqrt{3}}$	1	$\sqrt{3}$	∞
cot	∞	$\sqrt{3}$	1	$\frac{1}{\sqrt{3}}$	0
sec	1	$\frac{2}{\sqrt{3}}$	$\sqrt{2}$	2	∞
cosec	∞	2	$\sqrt{2}$	$\frac{2}{\sqrt{3}}$	1

LOGARITHMS

	0	1	2	3	4	5	6	7	8	9	Mean Differences								
											1	2	3	4	5	6	7	8	9
10	0000	0043	0086	0128	0170	0212	0253	0294	0334	0374	4	8	12	17	21	25	29	33	37
11	0414	0453	0492	0531	0569	0607	0645	0682	0719	0755	4	8	11	15	19	23	26	30	34
12	0792	0828	0864	0899	0934	0969	1004	1038	1072	1106	3	7	10	14	17	21	24	28	31
13	1139	1173	1206	1239	1271	1303	1335	1367	1399	1430	3	6	10	13	16	19	23	26	29
14	1461	1492	1523	1553	1584	1614	1644	1673	1703	1732	3	6	9	12	15	18	21	24	27
15	1761	1790	1818	1847	1875	1903	1931	1959	1987	2014	3	6	8	11	14	17	20	22	25
16	2041	2068	2095	2122	2148	2175	2201	2227	2253	2279	3	5	8	11	13	16	18	21	24
17	2304	2330	2355	2380	2405	2430	2455	2480	2504	2529	2	5	7	10	12	15	17	20	22
18	2553	2577	2601	2625	2648	2672	2695	2718	2742	2765	2	5	7	9	12	14	16	19	21
19	2788	2810	2833	2856	2878	2900	2923	2945	2967	2989	2	4	7	9	11	13	16	18	20
20	3010	3032	3054	3075	3096	3118	3139	3160	3181	3201	2	4	6	8	11	13	15	17	19
21	3222	3243	3263	3284	3304	3324	3345	3365	3385	3404	2	4	6	8	10	12	14	16	18
22	3424	3444	3464	3483	3502	3522	3541	3560	3579	3598	2	4	6	8	10	12	14	15	17
23	3617	3636	3655	3674	3692	3711	3729	3747	3766	3784	2	4	6	7	9	11	13	15	17
24	3802	3820	3838	3856	3874	3892	3909	3927	3945	3962	2	4	5	7	9	11	12	14	16
25	3979	3997	4014	4031	4048	4065	4082	4099	4116	4133	2	3	5	7	9	10	12	14	15
26	4150	4166	4183	4200	4216	4232	4249	4265	4281	4298	2	3	5	7	8	10	11	13	15
27	4314	4330	4346	4362	4378	4393	4409	4425	4440	4456	2	3	5	6	8	9	11	13	14
28	4472	4487	4502	4518	4533	4548	4564	4579	4594	4609	2	3	5	6	8	9	11	12	14
29	4624	4639	4654	4669	4683	4698	4713	4728	4742	4757	1	3	4	6	7	9	10	12	13
30	4771	4786	4800	4814	4829	4843	4857	4871	4886	4900	1	3	4	6	7	9	10	11	13
31	4914	4928	4942	4955	4969	4983	4997	5011	5024	5038	1	3	4	6	7	8	10	11	12
32	5051	5065	5079	5092	5105	5119	5132	5145	5159	5172	1	3	4	5	7	8	9	11	12
33	5185	5198	5211	5224	5237	5250	5263	5276	5289	5302	1	3	4	5	6	8	9	10	12
34	5315	5328	5340	5353	5366	5378	5391	5403	5416	5428	1	3	4	5	6	8	9	10	11
35	5441	5453	5465	5478	5490	5502	5514	5527	5539	5551	1	2	4	5	6	7	9	10	11
36	5563	5575	5587	5599	5611	5623	5635	5647	5658	5670	1	2	4	5	6	7	8	10	11
37	5682	5694	5705	5717	5729	5740	5752	5763	5775	5786	1	2	3	5	6	7	8	9	10
38	5798	5809	5821	5832	5843	5855	5866	5877	5888	5899	1	2	3	5	6	7	8	9	10
39	5911	5922	5933	5944	5955	5966	5977	5988	5999	6010	1	2	3	4	5	7	8	9	10
40	6021	6031	6042	6053	6064	6075	6085	6096	6107	6117	1	2	3	4	5	6	8	9	10
41	6128	6138	6149	6160	6170	6180	6191	6201	6212	6222	1	2	3	4	5	6	7	8	9
42	6232	6243	6253	6263	6274	6284	6294	6304	6314	6325	1	2	3	4	5	6	7	8	9
43	6335	6345	6355	6365	6375	6385	6395	6405	6415	6425	1	2	3	4	5	6	7	8	9
44	6435	6444	6454	6464	6474	6484	6493	6503	6513	6522	1	2	3	4	5	6	7	8	9
45	6532	6542	6551	6561	6571	6580	6590	6599	6609	6618	1	2	3	4	5	6	7	8	9
46	6628	6637	6646	6656	6665	6675	6684	6693	6702	6712	1	2	3	4	5	6	7	7	8
47	6721	6730	6739	6749	6758	6767	6776	6785	6794	6803	1	2	3	4	5	5	6	7	8
48	6812	6821	6830	6839	6848	6857	6866	6875	6884	6893	1	2	3	4	4	5	6	7	8
49	6902	6911	6920	6928	6937	6946	6955	6964	6972	6981	1	2	3	4	4	5	6	7	8
50	6990	6998	7007	7016	7024	7033	7042	7050	7059	7067	1	2	3	3	4	5	6	7	8
51	7076	7084	7093	7101	7110	7118	7126	7135	7143	7152	1	2	3	3	4	5	6	7	8
52	7160	7168	7177	7185	7193	7202	7210	7218	7226	7235	1	2	2	3	4	5	6	7	7
53	7243	7251	7259	7267	7275	7284	7292	7300	7308	7316	1	2	2	3	4	5	6	6	7
54	7324	7332	7340	7348	7356	7364	7372	7380	7388	7396	1	2	2	3	4	5	6	6	7

No.	**log**		**No.**	**log**
$\pi = 3.14159$	0.49715	$\ln x = \log_e x = (1/M) = \log_{10} x$	$(1/M) = 2.30259$	0.36222
$e = 2.71828$	0.43429	$\log x = \log_{10} x = M \log_e x$	$M = 0.43429$	$\bar{1}.63778$

LOGARITHMS

	0	1	2	3	4	5	6	7	8	9	Mean Differences								
											1	2	3	4	5	6	7	8	9
55	7404	7412	7419	7427	7435	7443	7451	7459	7466	7474	1	2	2	3	4	5	5	6	7
56	7482	7490	7497	7505	7513	7520	7528	7536	7543	7551	1	2	2	3	4	5	5	6	7
57	7559	7566	7574	7582	7589	7597	7604	7612	7619	7627	1	2	2	3	4	5	5	6	7
58	7634	7642	7649	7657	7664	7672	7679	7686	7694	7701	1	1	2	3	4	4	5	6	7
59	7709	7716	7723	7731	7738	7745	7752	7760	7767	7774	1	1	2	3	4	4	5	6	7
60	7782	7789	7796	7803	7810	7818	7825	7832	7839	7846	1	1	2	3	4	4	5	6	6
61	7853	7860	7868	7875	7882	7889	7896	7903	7910	7917	1	1	2	3	4	4	5	6	6
62	7924	7931	7938	7945	7952	7959	7966	7973	7980	7987	1	1	2	3	3	4	5	6	6
63	7993	8000	8007	8014	8021	8028	8035	8041	8048	8055	1	1	2	3	3	4	5	5	6
64	8062	8069	8075	8082	8089	8096	8102	8109	8116	8122	1	1	2	3	3	4	5	5	6
65	8129	8136	8142	8149	8156	8162	8169	8176	8182	8189	1	1	2	3	3	4	5	5	6
66	8195	8202	8209	8215	8222	8228	8235	8241	8248	8254	1	1	2	3	3	4	5	5	6
67	8261	8267	8274	8280	8287	8293	8299	8306	8312	8319	1	1	2	3	3	4	5	5	6
68	8325	8331	8338	8344	8351	8357	8363	8370	8376	8382	1	1	2	3	3	4	4	5	6
69	8388	8395	8401	8407	8414	8420	8426	8432	8439	8445	1	1	2	2	3	4	4	5	6
70	8451	8457	8463	8470	8476	8482	8488	8494	8500	8506	1	1	2	2	3	4	4	5	6
71	8513	8519	8525	8531	8537	8543	8549	8555	8561	8567	1	1	2	2	3	4	4	5	5
72	8573	8579	8585	8591	8597	8603	8609	8615	8621	8627	1	1	2	2	3	4	4	5	5
73	8633	8639	8645	8651	8657	8663	8669	8675	8681	8686	1	1	2	2	3	4	4	5	5
74	8692	8698	8704	8710	8716	8722	8727	8733	8739	8745	1	1	2	2	3	4	4	5	5
75	8751	8756	8762	8768	8774	8779	8785	8791	8797	8802	1	1	2	2	3	3	4	5	5
76	8808	8814	8820	8825	8831	8837	8842	8848	8854	8859	1	1	2	2	3	3	4	5	5
77	8865	8871	8876	8882	8887	8893	8899	8904	8910	8915	1	1	2	2	3	3	4	4	5
78	8921	8927	8932	8938	8943	8949	8954	8960	8965	8971	1	1	2	2	3	3	4	4	5
79	8976	8982	8987	8993	8998	9004	9009	9015	9020	9025	1	1	2	2	3	3	4	4	5
80	9031	9036	9042	9047	9053	9058	9063	9069	9074	9079	1	1	2	2	3	3	4	4	5
81	9085	9090	9096	9101	9106	9112	9117	9122	9128	9133	1	1	2	2	3	3	4	4	5
82	9138	9143	9149	9154	9159	9165	9170	9175	9180	9186	1	1	2	2	3	3	4	4	5
83	9191	9196	9201	9206	9212	9217	9222	9227	9232	9238	1	1	2	2	3	3	4	4	5
84	9243	9248	9253	9258	9263	9269	9274	9279	9284	9289	1	1	2	2	3	3	4	4	5
85	9294	9299	9304	9309	9315	9320	9325	9330	9335	9340	1	1	2	2	3	3	4	4	5
86	9345	9350	9355	9360	9365	9370	9375	9380	9385	9390	1	1	2	2	3	3	4	4	5
87	9395	9400	9405	9410	9415	9420	9425	9430	9435	9440	0	1	1	2	2	3	3	4	4
88	9445	9450	9455	9460	9465	9469	9474	9479	9484	9489	0	1	1	2	2	3	3	4	4
89	9494	9499	9504	9509	9513	9518	9523	9528	9533	9538	0	1	1	2	2	3	3	4	4
90	9542	9547	9552	9557	9562	9566	9571	9576	9581	9586	0	1	1	2	2	3	3	4	4
91	9590	9595	9600	9605	9609	9614	9619	9624	9628	9633	0	1	1	2	2	3	3	4	4
92	9638	9643	9647	9652	9657	9661	9666	9671	9675	9680	0	1	1	2	2	3	3	4	4
93	9685	9689	9694	9699	9703	9708	9713	9717	9722	9727	0	1	1	2	2	3	3	4	4
94	9731	9736	9741	9745	9750	9754	9759	9763	9768	9773	0	1	1	2	2	3	3	4	4
95	9777	9782	9786	9791	9795	9800	9805	9809	9814	9818	0	1	1	2	2	3	3	4	4
96	9823	9827	9832	9836	9841	9845	9850	9854	9859	9863	0	1	1	2	2	3	3	4	4
97	9868	9872	9877	9881	9886	9890	9894	9899	9903	9908	0	1	1	2	2	3	3	4	4
98	9912	9917	9921	9926	9930	9934	9939	9943	9948	9952	0	1	1	2	2	3	3	4	4
99	9956	9961	9965	9969	9974	9978	9983	9987	9991	9996	0	1	1	2	2	3	3	3	4

p	1	2	3	4	5	6	7	8	9	10
$\log e^{p}$	0.4343	0.8686	1.3029	1.7372	2.1715	2.6058	3.0401	3.4744	3.9087	4.3429
$\log e^{-p}$	$\bar{1}.5657$	$\bar{1}.1314$	$\bar{2}.6971$	$\bar{2}.2628$	$\bar{3}.8285$	$\bar{3}.3942$	$\bar{4}.9599$	$\bar{4}.5256$	$\bar{4}.0913$	$\bar{5}.6571$

ANTILOGARITHMS

	0	1	2	3	4	5	6	7	8	9	Mean Differences								
											1	2	3	4	5	6	7	8	9
.00	1000	1002	1005	1007	1009	1012	1014	1016	1019	1021	0	0	1	1	1	1	2	2	2
.01	1023	1026	1028	1030	1033	1035	1038	1040	1042	1045	0	0	1	1	1	1	2	2	2
.02	1047	1050	1052	1054	1057	1059	1062	1064	1067	1069	0	0	1	1	1	1	2	2	2
.03	1072	1074	1076	1079	1081	1084	1086	1089	1091	1094	0	0	1	1	1	1	2	2	2
.04	1096	1099	1102	1104	1107	1109	1112	1114	1117	1119	0	1	1	1	1	2	2	2	2
.05	1122	1125	1127	1130	1132	1135	1138	1140	1143	1146	0	1	1	1	1	2	2	2	2
.06	1148	1151	1153	1156	1159	1161	1164	1167	1169	1172	0	1	1	1	1	2	2	2	2
.07	1175	1178	1180	1183	1186	1189	1191	1194	1197	1199	0	1	1	1	1	2	2	2	2
.08	1202	1205	1208	1211	1213	1216	1219	1222	1225	1227	0	1	1	1	1	2	2	2	3
.09	1230	1233	1236	1239	1242	1245	1247	1250	1253	1256	0	1	1	1	1	2	2	2	3
.10	1259	1262	1265	1268	1271	1274	1276	1279	1282	1285	0	1	1	1	1	2	2	2	3
.11	1288	1291	1294	1297	1300	1303	1306	1309	1312	1315	0	1	1	1	2	2	2	2	3
.12	1318	1321	1324	1327	1330	1334	1337	1340	1343	1346	0	1	1	1	2	2	2	2	3
.13	1349	1352	1355	1358	1361	1365	1368	1371	1374	1377	0	1	1	1	2	2	2	3	3
.14	1380	1384	1387	1390	1393	1396	1400	1403	1406	1409	0	1	1	1	2	2	2	3	3
.15	1413	1416	1419	1422	1426	1429	1432	1435	1439	1442	0	1	1	1	2	2	2	3	3
.16	1445	1449	1452	1455	1459	1462	1466	1469	1472	1476	0	1	1	1	2	2	2	3	3
.17	1479	1483	1486	1489	1493	1496	1500	1503	1507	1510	0	1	1	1	2	2	2	3	3
.18	1514	1517	1521	1524	1528	1531	1535	1538	1542	1545	0	1	1	1	2	2	2	3	3
.19	1549	1552	1556	1560	1563	1567	1570	1574	1578	1581	0	1	1	1	2	2	3	3	3
.20	1585	1589	1592	1596	1600	1603	1607	1611	1614	1618	0	1	1	1	2	2	3	3	3
.21	1622	1626	1629	1633	1637	1641	1644	1648	1652	1656	0	1	1	2	2	2	3	3	3
.22	1660	1663	1667	1671	1675	1679	1683	1687	1690	1694	0	1	1	2	2	2	3	3	3
.23	1698	1702	1706	1710	1714	1718	1722	1726	1730	1734	0	1	1	2	2	2	3	3	4
.24	1738	1742	1746	1750	1754	1758	1762	1766	1770	1774	0	1	1	2	2	2	3	3	4
.25	1778	1782	1786	1791	1795	1799	1803	1807	1811	1816	0	1	1	2	2	2	3	3	4
.26	1820	1824	1828	1832	1837	1841	1845	1849	1854	1858	0	1	1	2	2	3	3	3	4
.27	1862	1866	1871	1875	1879	1884	1888	1892	1897	1901	0	1	1	2	2	3	3	3	4
.28	1905	1910	1914	1919	1923	1928	1932	1936	1941	1945	0	1	1	2	2	3	3	4	4
.29	1950	1954	1959	1963	1968	1972	1977	1982	1986	1991	0	1	1	2	2	3	3	4	4
.30	1995	2000	2004	2009	2014	2018	2023	2028	2032	2037	0	1	1	2	2	3	3	4	4
.31	2042	2046	2051	2056	2061	2065	2070	2075	2080	2084	0	1	1	2	2	3	3	4	4
.32	2089	2094	2099	2104	2109	2113	2118	2123	2128	2133	0	1	1	2	2	3	3	4	4
.33	2138	2143	2148	2153	2158	2163	2168	2173	2178	2183	0	1	1	2	2	3	3	4	4
.34	2188	2193	2198	2203	2208	2213	2218	2223	2228	2234	1	1	2	2	3	3	4	4	5
.35	2239	2244	2249	2254	2259	2265	2270	2275	2280	2286	1	1	2	2	3	3	4	4	5
.36	2291	2296	2301	2307	2312	2317	2323	2328	2333	2339	1	1	2	2	3	3	4	4	5
.37	2344	2350	2355	2360	2366	2371	2377	2382	2388	2393	1	1	2	2	3	3	4	4	5
.38	2399	2404	2410	2415	2421	2427	2432	2438	2443	2449	1	1	2	2	3	3	4	4	5
.39	2455	2460	2466	2472	2477	2483	2489	2495	2500	2506	1	1	2	2	3	3	4	5	5
.40	2512	2518	2523	2529	2535	2541	2547	2553	2559	2564	1	1	2	2	3	4	4	5	5
.41	2570	2576	2582	2588	2594	2600	2606	2612	2618	2624	1	1	2	2	3	4	4	5	5
.42	2630	2636	2642	2649	2655	2661	2667	2673	2679	2685	1	1	2	2	3	4	4	5	6
.43	2692	2698	2704	2710	2716	2723	2729	2735	2742	2748	1	1	2	3	3	4	4	5	6
.44	2754	2761	2767	2773	2780	2786	2793	2799	2805	2812	1	1	2	3	3	4	4	5	6
.45	2818	2825	2831	2838	2844	2851	2858	2864	2871	2877	1	1	2	3	3	4	5	5	6
.46	2884	2891	2897	2904	2911	2917	2924	2931	2938	2944	1	1	2	3	3	4	5	5	6
.47	2951	2958	2965	2972	2979	2985	2992	2999	3006	3013	1	1	2	3	3	4	5	5	6
.48	3020	3027	3034	3041	3048	3055	3062	3069	3076	3083	1	1	2	3	4	4	5	6	6
.49	3090	3097	3105	3112	3119	3126	3133	3141	3148	3155	1	1	2	3	4	4	5	6	6

ANTILOGARITHMS

	0	1	2	3	4	5	6	7	8	9	Mean Differences								
											1	2	3	4	5	6	7	8	9
.50	3162	3170	3177	3184	3192	3199	3206	3214	3221	3228	1	1	2	3	4	4	5	6	7
.51	3236	3243	3251	3258	3266	3273	3281	3289	3296	3304	1	2	2	3	4	5	5	6	7
.52	3311	3319	3327	3334	3342	3350	3357	3365	3373	3381	1	2	2	3	4	5	5	6	7
.53	3388	3396	3404	3412	3420	3428	3436	3443	3451	3459	1	2	2	3	4	5	6	6	7
.54	3467	3475	3483	3491	3499	3508	3516	3524	3532	3540	1	2	2	3	4	5	6	6	7
.55	3548	3556	3565	3573	3581	3589	3597	3606	3614	3622	1	2	2	3	4	5	6	7	7
.56	3631	3639	3648	3656	3664	3673	3681	3690	3698	3707	1	2	3	3	4	5	6	7	8
.57	3715	3724	3733	3741	3750	3758	3767	3776	3784	3793	1	2	3	3	4	5	6	7	8
.58	3802	3811	3819	3828	3837	3846	3855	3864	3873	3882	1	2	3	4	4	5	6	7	8
.59	3890	3899	3908	3917	3926	3936	3945	3954	3963	3972	1	2	3	4	5	5	6	7	8
.60	3981	3990	3999	4009	4018	4027	4036	4046	4055	4064	1	2	3	4	5	6	6	7	8
.61	4074	4083	4093	4102	4111	4121	4130	4140	4150	4159	1	2	3	4	5	6	7	8	9
.62	4169	4178	4188	4198	4207	4217	4227	4236	4246	4256	1	2	3	4	5	6	7	8	9
.63	4266	4276	4285	4295	4305	4315	4325	4335	4345	4355	1	2	3	4	5	6	7	8	9
.64	4365	4375	4385	4395	4406	4416	4426	4436	4446	4457	1	2	3	4	5	6	7	8	9
.65	4467	4477	4487	4498	4508	4519	4529	4539	4550	4560	1	2	3	4	5	6	7	8	9
.66	4571	4581	4592	4603	4613	4624	4634	4645	4656	4667	1	2	3	4	5	6	7	9	10
.67	4677	4688	4699	4710	4721	4732	4742	4753	4764	4775	1	2	3	4	5	7	8	9	10
.68	4786	4797	4808	4819	4831	4842	4853	4864	4875	4887	1	2	3	4	6	7	8	9	10
.69	4898	4909	4920	4932	4943	4955	4966	4977	4989	5000	1	2	3	5	6	7	8	9	10
.70	5012	5023	5035	5047	5058	5070	5082	5093	5105	5117	1	2	4	5	6	7	8	9	11
.71	5129	5140	5152	5164	5176	5188	5200	5212	5224	5236	1	2	4	5	6	7	8	10	11
.72	5248	5260	5272	5284	5297	5309	5321	5333	5346	5358	1	2	4	5	6	7	9	10	11
.73	5370	5383	5395	5408	5420	5433	5445	5458	5470	5483	1	3	4	5	6	8	9	10	11
.74	5495	5508	5521	5534	5546	5559	5572	5585	5598	5610	1	3	4	5	6	8	9	10	12
.75	5623	5636	5649	5662	5675	5689	5702	5715	5728	5741	1	3	4	5	7	8	9	10	12
.76	5754	5768	5781	5794	5808	5821	5834	5848	5861	5875	1	3	4	5	7	8	9	11	12
.77	5888	5902	5916	5929	5943	5957	5970	5984	5998	6012	1	3	4	5	7	8	10	11	12
.78	6026	6039	6053	6067	6081	6095	6109	6124	6138	6152	1	3	4	6	7	8	10	11	13
.79	6166	6180	6194	6209	6223	6237	6252	6266	6281	6295	1	3	4	6	7	9	10	11	13
.80	6310	6324	6339	6353	6368	6383	6397	6412	6427	6442	1	3	4	6	7	9	10	12	13
.81	6457	6471	6486	6501	6516	6531	6546	6561	6577	6592	2	3	5	6	8	9	11	12	14
.82	6607	6622	6637	6653	6668	6683	6699	6714	6730	6745	2	3	5	6	8	9	11	12	14
.83	6761	6776	6792	6808	6823	6839	6855	6871	6887	6902	2	3	5	6	8	9	11	13	14
.84	6918	6934	6950	6966	6982	6998	7015	7031	7047	7063	2	3	5	6	8	10	11	13	15
.85	7079	7096	7112	7129	7145	7161	7178	7194	7211	7228	2	3	5	7	8	10	12	13	15
.86	7244	7261	7278	7295	7311	7328	7345	7362	7379	7396	2	3	5	7	8	10	12	13	15
.87	7413	7430	7447	7464	7482	7499	7516	7534	7551	7568	2	3	5	7	9	10	12	14	16
.88	7586	7603	7621	7638	7656	7674	7691	7709	7727	7745	2	4	5	7	9	11	12	14	16
.89	7762	7780	7798	7816	7834	7852	7870	7889	7907	7925	2	4	5	7	9	11	13	14	16
.90	7943	7962	7980	7998	8017	8035	8054	8072	8091	8110	2	4	6	7	9	11	13	15	17
.91	8128	8147	8166	8185	8204	8222	8241	8260	8279	8299	2	4	6	8	9	11	13	15	17
.92	8318	8337	8356	8375	8395	8414	8433	8453	8472	8492	2	4	6	8	10	12	14	15	17
.93	8511	8531	8551	8570	8590	8610	8630	8650	8670	8690	2	4	6	8	10	12	14	16	18
.94	8710	8730	8750	8770	8790	8810	8831	8851	8872	8892	2	4	6	8	10	12	14	16	18
.95	8913	8933	8954	8974	8995	9016	9036	9057	9078	9099	2	4	6	8	10	12	15	17	19
.96	9120	9141	9162	9183	9204	9226	9247	9268	9290	9311	2	4	6	8	11	13	15	17	19
.97	9333	9354	9376	9397	9419	9441	9462	9484	9506	9528	2	4	7	9	11	13	15	17	20
.98	9550	9572	9594	9616	9638	9661	9683	9705	9727	9750	2	4	7	9	11	13	16	18	20
.99	9772	9795	9817	9840	9863	9886	9908	9931	9954	9977	2	5	7	9	11	14	16	18	20

Natural Sines

Degrees	0′ 0.0°	6′ 0.1°	12′ 0.2°	18′ 0.3°	24′ 0.4°	30′ 0.5°	36′ 0.6°	42′ 0.7°	48′ 0.8°	54′ 0.9°	Mean Differences 1′	2′	3′	4′	5′
0°	.0000	0017	0035	0052	0070	0087	0105	0122	0140	0157	3	6	9	12	15
1	.0175	0192	0209	0227	0244	0262	0279	0297	0314	0332	3	6	9	12	15
2	.0349	0366	0384	0401	0419	0436	0454	0471	0488	0506	3	6	9	12	15
3	.0523	0541	0558	0576	0593	0610	0628	0645	0663	0680	3	6	9	12	15
4	.0698	0715	0732	0750	0767	0785	0802	0819	0837	0854	3	6	9	12	14
5	.0872	0889	0906	0924	0941	0958	0976	0993	1011	1028	3	6	9	12	14
6	.1045	1063	1080	1097	1115	1132	1149	1167	1184	1201	3	6	9	12	14
7	.1219	1236	1253	1271	1288	1305	1323	1340	1357	1374	3	6	9	12	14
8	.1392	1409	1426	1444	1461	1478	1495	1513	1530	1547	3	6	9	12	14
9	.1564	1582	1599	1616	1633	1650	1668	1685	1702	1719	3	6	9	12	14
10°	.1736	1754	1771	1788	1805	1822	1840	1857	1874	1891	3	6	9	11	14
11	.1908	1925	1942	1959	1977	1994	2011	2028	2045	2062	3	6	9	11	14
12	.2079	2096	2113	2130	2147	2164	2181	2198	2215	2233	3	6	9	11	14
13	.2250	2267	2284	2300	2317	2334	2351	2368	2385	2402	3	6	8	11	14
14	.2419	2436	2453	2470	2487	2504	2521	2538	2554	2571	3	6	8	11	14
15	.2588	2605	2622	2639	2656	2672	2689	2706	2723	2740	3	6	8	11	14
16	.2756	2773	2790	2807	2823	2840	2857	2874	2890	2907	3	6	8	11	14
17	.2924	2940	2957	2974	2990	3007	3024	3040	3057	3074	3	6	8	11	14
18	.3090	3107	3123	3140	3156	3173	3190	3206	3223	3239	3	6	8	11	14
19	.3256	3272	3289	3305	3322	3338	3355	3371	3387	3404	3	5	8	11	14
20°	.3420	3437	3453	3469	3486	3502	3518	3535	3551	3567	3	5	8	11	14
21	.3584	3600	3616	3633	3649	3665	3681	3697	3714	3730	3	5	8	11	14
22	.3746	3762	3778	3795	3811	3827	3843	3859	3875	3891	3	5	8	11	14
23	.3907	3923	3939	3955	3971	3987	4003	4019	4035	4051	3	5	8	11	14
24	.4067	4083	4099	4115	4131	4147	4163	4179	4195	4210	3	5	8	11	13
25	.4226	4242	4258	4274	4289	4305	4321	4337	4352	4368	3	5	8	11	13
26	.4384	4399	4415	4431	4446	4462	4478	4493	4509	4524	3	5	8	10	13
27	.4540	4555	4571	4586	4602	4617	4633	4648	4664	4679	3	5	8	10	13
28	.4695	4710	4726	4741	4756	4772	4787	4802	4818	4833	3	5	8	10	13
29	.4848	4863	4879	4894	4909	4924	4939	4955	4970	4985	3	5	8	10	13
30°	.5000	5015	5030	5045	5060	5075	5090	5105	5120	5135	3	5	8	10	13
31	.5150	5165	5180	5195	5210	5225	5240	5255	5270	5284	2	5	7	10	12
32	.5299	5314	5329	5344	5358	5373	5388	5402	5417	5432	2	5	7	10	12
33	.5446	5461	5476	5490	5505	5519	5534	5548	5563	5577	2	5	7	10	12
34	.5592	5606	5621	5635	5650	5664	5678	5693	5707	5721	2	5	7	10	12
35	.5736	5750	5764	5779	5793	5807	5821	5835	5850	5864	2	5	7	9	12
36	.5878	5892	5906	5920	5934	5948	5962	5976	5990	6004	2	5	7	9	12
37	.6018	6032	6046	6060	6074	6088	6101	6115	6129	6143	2	5	7	9	12
38	.6157	6170	6184	6198	6211	6225	6239	6252	6266	6280	2	5	7	9	11
39	.6293	6307	6320	6334	6347	6361	6374	6388	6401	6414	2	4	7	9	11
40°	.6428	6441	6455	6468	6481	6494	6508	6521	6534	6547	2	4	7	9	11
41	.6561	6574	6587	6600	6613	6626	6639	6652	6665	6678	2	4	7	9	11
42	.6691	6704	6717	6730	6743	6756	6769	6782	6794	6807	2	4	6	9	11
43	.6820	6833	6845	6858	6871	6884	6896	6909	6921	6934	2	4	6	8	11
44	.6947	6959	6972	6984	6997	7009	7022	7034	7046	7059	2	4	6	8	10

Natural Sines

Degrees	0′ 0.0°	6′ 0.1°	12′ 0.2°	18′ 0.3°	24′ 0.4°	30′ 0.5°	36′ 0.6°	42′ 0.7°	48′ 0.8°	54′ 0.9°	Mean Differences 1′	2′	3′	4′	5′
45°	.7071	7083	7096	7108	7120	7133	7145	7157	7169	7181	2	4	6	8	10
46	.7193	7206	7218	7230	7242	7254	7266	7278	7290	7302	2	4	6	8	10
47	.7314	7325	7337	7349	7361	7373	7385	7396	7408	7420	2	4	6	8	10
48	.7431	7443	7455	7466	7478	7490	7501	7513	7524	7536	2	4	6	8	10
49	.7547	7559	7570	7581	7593	7604	7615	7627	7638	7649	2	4	6	8	9
50°	.7660	7672	7683	7694	7705	7716	7727	7738	7749	7760	2	4	6	7	9
51	.7771	7782	7793	7804	7815	7826	7837	7848	7859	7869	2	4	5	7	9
52	.7880	7891	7902	7912	7923	7934	7944	7955	7965	7976	2	4	5	7	9
53	.7986	7997	8007	8018	8028	8039	8049	8059	8070	8080	2	3	5	7	9
54	.8090	8100	8111	8121	8131	8141	8151	8161	8171	8181	2	3	5	7	8
55	.8192	8202	8211	8221	8231	8241	8251	8261	8271	8281	2	3	5	7	8
56	.8290	8300	8310	8320	8329	8339	8348	8358	8368	8377	2	3	5	6	8
57	.8387	8396	8406	8415	8425	8434	8443	8453	8462	8471	2	3	5	6	8
58	.8480	8490	8499	8508	8517	8526	8536	8545	8554	8563	2	3	5	6	8
59	.8572	8581	8590	8599	8607	8616	8625	8634	8643	8652	1	3	4	6	7
60°	.8660	8669	8678	8686	8695	8704	8712	8721	8729	8738	1	3	4	6	7
61	.8746	8755	8763	8771	8780	8788	8796	8805	8813	8821	1	3	4	6	7
62	.8829	8838	8846	8854	8862	8870	8878	8886	8894	8902	1	3	4	5	7
63	.8910	8918	8926	8934	8942	8949	8957	8965	8973	8980	1	3	4	5	6
64	.8988	8996	9003	9011	9018	9026	9033	9041	9048	9056	1	3	4	5	6
65	.9063	9070	9078	9085	9092	9100	9107	9114	9121	9128	1	2	4	5	6
66	.9135	9143	9150	9157	9164	9171	9178	9184	9191	9198	1	2	3	5	6
67	.9205	9212	9219	9225	9232	9239	9245	9252	9259	9265	1	2	3	4	6
68	.9272	9278	9285	9291	9298	9304	9311	9317	9323	9330	1	2	3	4	5
69	.9336	9342	9348	9354	9361	9367	9373	9379	9385	9391	1	2	3	4	5
70°	.9397	9403	9409	9415	9421	9426	9432	9438	9444	9449	1	2	3	4	5
71	.9455	9461	9466	9472	9478	9483	9489	9494	9500	9505	1	2	3	4	5
72	.9511	9516	9521	9527	9532	9537	9542	9548	9553	9558	1	2	3	3	4
73	.9563	9568	9573	9578	9583	9588	9593	9598	9603	9608	1	2	2	3	4
74	.9613	9617	9622	9627	9632	9636	9641	9646	9650	9655	1	2	2	3	4
75	.9659	9664	9668	9673	9677	9681	9686	9690	9694	9699	1	1	2	3	4
76	.9703	9707	9711	9715	9720	9724	9728	9732	9736	9740	1	1	2	3	3
77	.9744	9748	9751	9755	9759	9763	9767	9770	9774	9778	1	1	2	3	3
78	.9781	9785	9789	9792	9796	9799	9803	9806	9810	9813	1	1	2	2	3
79	.9816	9820	9823	9826	9829	9833	9836	9839	9842	9845	1	1	2	2	3
80°	.9848	9851	9854	9857	9860	9863	9866	9869	9871	9874	0	1	1	2	2
81	.9877	9880	9882	9885	9888	9890	9893	9895	9898	9900	0	1	1	2	2
82	.9903	9905	9907	9910	9912	9914	9917	9919	9921	9923	0	1	1	2	2
83	.9925	9928	9930	9932	9934	9936	9938	9940	9942	9943	0	1	1	1	2
84	.9945	9947	9949	9951	9952	9954	9956	9957	9959	9960	0	1	1	1	2
85	.9962	9963	9965	9966	9968	9969	9971	9972	9973	9974	0	0	1	1	1
86	.9976	9977	9978	9979	9980	9981	9982	9983	9984	9985	0	0	1	1	1
87	.9986	9987	9988	9989	9990	9990	9991	9992	9993	9993	0	0	0	1	1
88	.9994	9995	9995	9996	9996	9997	9997	9997	9998	9998	0	0	0	0	0
89	.9998	9999	9999	9999	9999	1.000	1.000	1.000	1.000	1.000	0	0	0	0	0

Natural Cosines

[*N.B. – Subtract* Mean Differences]

Degrees	0′ 0.0°	6′ 0.1°	12′ 0.2°	18′ 0.3°	24′ 0.4°	30′ 0.5°	36′ 0.6°	42′ 0.7°	48′ 0.8°	54′ 0.9°	Mean Differences SUBTRACT 1′	 2′	 3′	 4′	 5′
0°	1.000	1.000	1.000	1.000	1.000	1.000	9999	9999	9999	9999	0	0	0	0	0
1	.9998	9998	9998	9997	9997	9997	9996	9996	9995	9995	0	0	0	0	0
2	.9994	9993	9993	9992	9991	9990	9990	9989	9988	9987	0	0	0	1	1
3	.9986	9985	9984	9983	9982	9981	9980	9979	9978	9977	0	0	1	1	1
4	.9976	9974	9973	9972	9971	9969	9968	9966	9965	9963	0	0	1	1	1
5	.9962	9960	9959	9957	9956	9954	9952	9951	9949	9947	0	1	1	1	2
6	.9945	9943	9942	9940	9938	9936	9934	9932	9930	9928	0	1	1	1	2
7	.9925	9923	9921	9919	9917	9914	9912	9910	9907	9905	0	1	1	2	2
8	.9903	9900	9898	9895	9893	9890	9888	9885	9882	9880	0	1	1	2	2
9	.9877	9874	9871	9869	9866	9863	9860	9857	9854	9851	0	1	1	2	2
10°	.9848	9845	9842	9839	9836	9833	9829	9826	9823	9820	1	1	2	2	3
11	.9816	9813	9810	9806	9803	9799	9796	9792	9789	9785	1	1	2	2	3
12	.9781	9778	9774	9770	9767	9763	9759	9755	9751	9748	1	1	2	3	3
13	.9744	9740	9736	9732	9728	9724	9720	9715	9711	9707	1	1	2	3	3
14	.9703	9699	9694	9690	9686	9681	9677	9673	9668	9664	1	1	2	3	4
15	.9659	9655	9650	9646	9641	9636	9632	9627	9622	9617	1	2	2	3	4
16	.9613	9608	9603	9598	9593	9588	9583	9578	9573	9568	1	2	2	3	4
17	.9563	9558	9553	9548	9542	9537	9532	9527	9521	9516	1	2	3	3	4
18	.9511	9505	9500	9494	9489	9483	9478	9472	9466	9461	1	2	3	4	5
19	.9455	9449	9444	9438	9432	9426	9421	9415	9409	9403	1	2	3	4	5
20°	.9397	9391	9385	9379	9373	9367	9361	9354	9348	9342	1	2	3	4	5
21	.9336	9330	9323	9317	9311	9304	9298	9291	9285	9278	1	2	3	4	5
22	.9272	9265	9259	9252	9245	9239	9232	9225	9219	9212	1	2	3	4	6
23	.9205	9198	9191	9184	9178	9171	9164	9157	9150	9143	1	2	3	5	6
24	.9135	9128	9121	9114	9107	9100	9092	9085	9078	9070	1	2	4	5	6
25	.9063	9056	9048	9041	9033	9026	9018	9011	9003	8996	1	3	4	5	6
26	.8988	8980	8973	8965	8957	8949	8942	8934	8926	8918	1	3	4	5	6
27	.8910	8902	8894	8886	8878	8870	8862	8854	8846	8838	1	3	4	5	7
28	.8829	8821	8813	8805	8796	8788	8780	8771	8763	8755	1	3	4	6	7
29	.8746	8738	8729	8721	8712	8704	8695	8686	8678	8669	1	3	4	6	7
30°	.8660	8652	8643	8634	8625	8616	8607	8599	8590	8581	1	3	4	6	7
31	.8572	8563	8554	8545	8536	8526	8517	8508	8499	8490	2	3	5	6	8
32	.8480	8471	8462	8453	8443	8434	8425	8415	8406	8396	2	3	5	6	8
33	.8387	8377	8368	8358	8348	8339	8329	8320	8310	8300	2	3	5	6	8
34	.8290	8281	8271	8261	8251	8241	8231	8221	8211	8202	2	3	5	7	8
35	.8192	8181	8171	8161	8151	8141	8131	8121	8111	8100	2	3	5	7	8
36	.8090	8080	8070	8059	8049	8039	8028	8018	8007	7997	2	3	5	7	9
37	.7986	7976	7965	7955	7944	7934	7923	7912	7902	7891	2	4	5	7	9
38	.7880	7869	7859	7848	7837	7826	7815	7804	7793	7782	2	4	5	7	9
39	.7771	7760	7749	7738	7727	7716	7705	7694	7683	7672	2	4	6	7	9
40°	.7660	7649	7638	7627	7615	7604	7593	7581	7570	7559	2	4	6	8	9
41	.7547	7536	7524	7513	7501	7490	7478	7466	7455	7443	2	4	6	8	10
42	.7431	7420	7408	7396	7385	7373	7361	7349	7337	7325	2	4	6	8	10
43	.7314	7302	7290	7278	7266	7254	7242	7230	7218	7206	2	4	6	8	10
44	.7193	7181	7169	7157	7145	7133	7120	7108	7096	7083	2	4	6	8	10

Natural Cosines

[*N.B. – Subtract* Mean Differences]

Degrees	0′	6′	12′	18′	24′	30′	36′	42′	48′	54′	Mean Differences SUBTRACT				
	0.0°	0.1°	0.2°	0.3°	0.4°	0.5°	0.6°	0.7°	0.8°	0.9°	1′	2′	3′	4′	5′
45°	.7071	7059	7046	7034	7022	7009	6997	6984	6972	6959	2	4	6	8	10
46	.6947	6934	6921	6909	6896	6884	6871	6858	6845	6833	2	4	6	9	11
47	.6820	6807	6794	6782	6769	6756	6743	6730	6717	6704	2	4	6	9	11
48	.6691	6678	6665	6652	6639	6626	6613	6600	6587	6574	2	4	7	9	11
49	.6561	6547	6534	6521	6508	6494	6481	6468	6455	6441	2	4	7	9	11
50°	.6428	6414	6401	6388	6374	6361	6347	6334	6320	6307	2	4	7	9	11
51	.6293	6280	6266	6252	6239	6225	6211	6198	6184	6170	2	5	7	9	11
52	.6157	6143	6129	6115	6101	6088	6074	6060	6046	6032	2	5	7	9	12
53	.6018	6004	5990	5976	5962	5948	5934	5920	5906	5892	2	5	7	9	12
54	.5878	5864	5850	5835	5821	5807	5793	5779	5764	5750	2	5	7	9	12
55	.5736	5721	5707	5693	5678	5664	5650	5635	5621	5606	2	5	7	10	12
56	.5592	5577	5563	5548	5534	5519	5505	5490	5476	5461	2	5	7	10	12
57	.5446	5432	5417	5402	5388	5373	5358	5344	5329	5314	2	5	7	10	12
58	.5299	5284	5270	5255	5240	5225	5210	5195	5180	5165	2	5	7	10	12
59	.5150	5135	5120	5105	5090	5075	5060	5045	5030	5015	3	5	8	10	13
60°	.5000	4985	4970	4955	4939	4924	4909	4894	4879	4863	3	5	8	10	13
61	.4848	4833	4818	4802	4787	4772	4756	4741	4726	4710	3	5	8	10	13
62	.4695	4679	4664	4648	4633	4617	4602	4586	4571	4555	3	5	8	10	13
63	.4540	4524	4509	4493	4478	4462	4446	4431	4415	4399	3	5	8	10	13
64	.4384	4368	4352	4337	4321	4305	4289	4274	4258	4242	3	5	8	11	13
65	.4226	4210	4195	4179	4163	4147	4131	4115	4099	4083	3	5	8	11	13
66	.4067	4051	4035	4019	4003	3987	3971	3955	3939	3923	3	5	8	11	14
67	.3907	3891	3875	3859	3843	3827	3811	3795	3778	3762	3	5	8	11	14
68	.3746	3730	3714	3697	3681	3665	3649	3633	3616	3600	3	5	8	11	14
69	.3584	3567	3551	3535	3518	3502	3486	3469	3453	3437	3	5	8	11	14
70°	.3420	3404	3387	3371	3355	3338	3322	3305	3289	3272	3	5	8	11	14
71	.3256	3239	3223	3206	3190	3173	3156	3140	3123	3107	3	6	8	11	14
72	.3090	3074	3057	3040	3024	3007	2990	2974	2957	2940	3	6	8	11	14
73	.2924	2907	2890	2874	2857	2840	2823	2807	2790	2773	3	6	8	11	14
74	.2756	2740	2723	2706	2689	2672	2656	2639	2622	2605	3	6	8	11	14
75	.2588	2571	2554	2538	2521	2504	2487	2470	2453	2436	3	6	8	11	14
76	.2419	2402	2385	2368	2351	2334	2317	2300	2284	2267	3	6	8	11	14
77	.2250	2233	2215	2198	2181	2164	2147	2130	2113	2096	3	6	9	11	14
78	.2079	2062	2045	2028	2011	1994	1977	1959	1942	1925	3	6	9	11	14
79	.1908	1891	1874	1857	1840	1822	1805	1788	1771	1754	3	6	9	11	14
80°	.1736	1719	1702	1685	1668	1650	1633	1616	1599	1582	3	6	9	12	14
81	.1564	1547	1530	1513	1495	1478	1461	1444	1426	1409	3	6	9	12	14
82	.1392	1374	1357	1340	1323	1305	1288	1271	1253	1236	3	6	9	12	14
83	.1219	1201	1184	1167	1149	1132	1115	1097	1080	1063	3	6	9	12	14
84	.1045	1028	1011	0993	0976	0958	0941	0924	0906	0889	3	6	9	12	14
85	.0872	0854	0837	0819	0802	0785	0767	0750	0732	0715	3	6	9	12	14
86	.0698	0680	0663	0645	0628	0610	0593	0576	0558	0541	3	6	9	12	15
87	.0523	0506	0488	0471	0454	0436	0419	0401	0384	0366	3	6	9	12	15
88	.0349	0332	0314	0297	0279	0262	0244	0227	0209	0192	3	6	9	12	15
89	.0175	0157	0140	0122	0105	0087	0070	0052	0035	0017	3	6	9	12	15

Natural Tangents

Degrees	0′ 0.0°	6′ 0.1°	12′ 0.2°	18′ 0.3°	24′ 0.4°	30′ 0.5°	36′ 0.6°	42′ 0.7°	48′ 0.8°	54′ 0.9°	Mean Differences 1′	2′	3′	4′	5′
0°	.0000	0017	0035	0052	0070	0087	0105	0122	0140	0157	3	6	9	12	15
1	.0175	0192	0209	0227	0244	0262	0279	0297	0314	0332	3	6	9	12	15
2	.0349	0367	0384	0402	0419	0437	0454	0472	0489	0507	3	6	9	12	15
3	.0524	0542	0559	0577	0594	0612	0629	0647	0664	0682	3	6	9	12	15
4	.0699	0717	0734	0752	0769	0787	0805	0822	0840	0857	3	6	9	12	15
5	.0875	0892	0910	0928	0945	0963	0981	0998	1016	1033	3	6	9	12	15
6	.1051	1069	1086	1104	1122	1139	1157	1175	1192	1210	3	6	9	12	15
7	.1228	1246	1263	1281	1299	1317	1334	1352	1370	1388	3	6	9	12	15
8	.1405	1423	1441	1459	1477	1495	1512	1530	1548	1566	3	6	9	12	15
9	.1584	1602	1620	1638	1655	1673	1691	1709	1727	1745	3	6	9	12	15
10°	.1763	1781	1799	1817	1835	1853	1871	1890	1908	1926	3	6	9	12	15
11	.1944	1962	1980	1998	2016	2035	2053	2071	2089	2107	3	6	9	12	15
12	.2126	2144	2162	2180	2199	2217	2235	2254	2272	2290	3	6	9	12	15
13	.2309	2327	2345	2364	2382	2401	2419	2438	2456	2475	3	6	9	12	15
14	.2493	2512	2530	2549	2568	2586	2605	2623	2642	2661	3	6	9	12	16
15	.2679	2698	2717	2736	2754	2773	2792	2811	2830	2849	3	6	9	13	16
16	.2867	2886	2905	2924	2943	2962	2981	3000	3019	3038	3	6	9	13	16
17	.3057	3076	3096	3115	3134	3153	3172	3191	3211	3230	3	6	10	13	16
18	.3249	3269	3288	3307	3327	3346	3365	3385	3404	3424	3	6	10	13	16
19	.3443	3463	3482	3502	3522	3541	3561	3581	3600	3620	3	7	10	13	16
20°	.3640	3659	3679	3699	3719	3739	3759	3779	3799	3819	3	7	10	13	17
21	.3839	3859	3879	3899	3919	3939	3959	3979	4000	4020	3	7	10	13	17
22	.4040	4061	4081	4101	4122	4142	4163	4183	4204	4224	3	7	10	14	17
23	.4245	4265	4286	4307	4327	4348	4369	4390	4411	4431	3	7	10	14	17
24	.4452	4473	4494	4515	4536	4557	4578	4599	4621	4642	4	7	11	14	18
25	.4663	4684	4706	4727	4748	4770	4791	4813	4834	4856	4	7	11	14	18
26	.4877	4899	4921	4942	4964	4986	5008	5029	5051	5073	4	7	11	15	18
27	.5095	5117	5139	5161	5184	5206	5228	5250	5272	5295	4	7	11	15	18
28	.5317	5340	5362	5384	5407	5430	5452	5475	5498	5520	4	8	11	15	19
29	.5543	5566	5589	5612	5635	5658	5681	5704	5727	5750	4	8	12	15	19
30°	.5774	5797	5820	5844	5867	5890	5914	5938	5961	5985	4	8	12	16	20
31	.6009	6032	6056	6080	6104	6128	6152	6176	6200	6224	4	8	12	16	20
32	.6249	6273	6297	6322	6346	6371	6395	6420	6445	6469	4	8	12	16	20
33	.6494	6519	6544	6569	6594	6619	6644	6669	6694	6720	4	8	13	17	21
34	.6745	6771	6796	6822	6847	6873	6899	6924	6950	6976	4	9	13	17	21
35	.7002	7028	7054	7080	7107	7133	7159	7186	7212	7239	4	9	13	18	22
36	.7265	7292	7319	7346	7373	7400	7427	7454	7481	7508	5	9	14	18	23
37	.7536	7563	7590	7618	7646	7673	7701	7729	7757	7785	5	9	14	18	23
38	.7813	7841	7869	7898	7926	7954	7983	8012	8040	8069	5	9	14	19	24
39	.8098	8127	8156	8185	8214	8243	8273	8302	8332	8361	5	10	15	20	24
40°	.8391	8421	8451	8481	8511	8541	8571	8601	8632	8662	5	10	15	20	25
41	.8693	8724	8754	8785	8816	8847	8878	8910	8941	8972	5	10	16	21	26
42	.9004	9036	9067	9099	9113	9163	9195	9228	9260	9293	5	11	16	21	27
43	.9325	9358	9391	9424	9457	9490	9523	9556	9590	9623	6	11	17	22	28
44	.9657	9691	9725	9759	9793	9827	9861	9896	9930	9965	6	11	17	23	29

Natural Tangents

Degrees	0′ 0.0°	6′ 0.1°	12′ 0.2°	18′ 0.3°	24′ 0.4°	30′ 0.5°	36′ 0.6°	42′ 0.7°	48′ 0.8°	54′ 0.9°	Mean Differences 1′	2′	3′	4′	5′
45°	1.0000	0035	0070	0105	0141	0176	0212	0247	0283	0319	6	12	18	24	30
46	1.0355	0392	0428	0464	0501	0538	0575	0612	0649	0686	6	12	18	25	31
47	1.0724	0761	0799	0837	0875	0913	0951	0990	1028	1067	6	13	19	25	32
48	1.1106	1145	1184	1224	1263	1303	1343	1383	1423	1463	7	13	20	27	33
49	1.1504	1544	1585	1626	1667	1708	1750	1792	1833	1875	7	14	21	28	34
50°	1.1918	1960	2002	2045	2088	2131	2174	2218	2261	2305	7	14	22	29	36
51	1.2349	2393	2437	2482	2527	2572	2617	2662	2708	2753	8	15	23	30	38
52	1.2799	2846	2892	2938	2985	3032	3079	3127	3175	3222	8	16	24	31	39
53	1.3270	3319	3367	3416	3465	3514	3564	3613	3663	3713	8	16	25	33	41
54	1.3764	3814	3865	3916	3968	4019	4071	4124	4176	4229	9	17	26	34	43
55	1.4281	4335	4388	4442	4496	4550	4605	4659	4715	4770	9	18	27	36	45
56	1.4826	4882	4938	4994	5051	5108	5166	5224	5282	5340	10	19	29	38	48
57	1.5399	5458	5517	5577	5637	5697	5757	5818	5880	5941	10	20	30	40	50
58	1.6003	6066	6128	6191	6255	6319	6383	6447	6512	6577	11	21	32	43	53
59	1.6643	6709	6775	6842	6909	6977	7045	7113	7182	7251	11	23	34	45	56
60°	1.7321	7391	7461	7532	7603	7675	7747	7820	7893	7966	12	24	36	48	60
61	1.8040	8115	8190	8265	8341	8418	8495	8572	8650	8728	13	26	38	51	64
62	1.8807	8887	8967	9047	9128	9210	9292	9375	9458	9542	14	27	41	55	68
63	1.9626	9711	9797	9883	9970	2.0057	2.0145	2.0233	2.0323	2.0413	15	29	44	58	73
64	2.0503	0594	0686	0778	0872	0965	1060	1155	1251	1348	16	31	47	63	78
65	2.1445	1543	1642	1742	1842	1943	2045	2148	2251	2355	17	34	51	68	85
66	2.2460	2566	2673	2781	2889	2998	3109	3220	3332	3445	18	37	55	73	92
67	2.3559	3673	3789	3906	4023	4142	4262	4383	4504	4627	20	40	60	79	99
68	2.4751	4876	5002	5129	5257	5386	5517	5649	5782	5916	22	43	65	87	108
69	2.6051	6187	6325	6464	6605	6746	6889	7034	7179	7326	24	47	71	95	119
70°	2.7475	7625	7776	7929	8083	8239	8397	8556	8716	8878	26	52	78	104	131
71	2.9042	9208	9375	9544	9714	9887	3.0061	3.0237	3.0415	3.0595	29	58	87	116	145
72	3.0777	0961	1146	1334	1524	1716	1910	2106	2305	2506	32	64	96	129	161
73	3.2709	2914	3122	3332	3544	3759	3977	4197	4420	4646	36	72	108	144	180
74	3.4874	5105	5339	5576	5816	6059	6305	6554	6806	7062	41	81	122	163	204
75	3.7321	7583	7848	8118	8391	8667	8947	9232	9520	9812	46	93	139	186	232
76	4.0108	0408	0713	1022	1335	1653	1976	2303	2635	2972	53	107	160	213	267
77	4.3315	3662	4015	4374	4737	5107	5483	5864	6252	6646					
78	4.7046	7453	7867	8288	8716	9152	9594	5.0045	5.0504	5.0970					
79	5.1446	1929	2422	2924	3435	3955	4486	5026	5578	6140					
80°	5.6713	7297	7894	8502	9124	9758	6.0405	6.1066	6.1742	6.2432					
81	6.3138	3859	4596	5350	6122	6912	7720	8548	9395	7.0264	*Mean* differences no longer sufficiently accurate.				
82	7.1154	2066	3002	3962	4947	5958	6996	8062	9158	8.0285					
83	8.1443	2636	3863	5126	6427	7769	9152	9.0579	9.2052	9.0372					
84	9.5144	9.677	9.845	10.02	10.20	10.39	10.58	10.78	10.99	11.20					
85	11.43	11.66	11.91	12.16	12.43	12.71	13.00	13.30	13.62	13.95					
86	14.30	14.57	15.06	15.46	15.89	16.35	16.83	17.34	17.89	18.46					
87	19.08	19.74	20.45	21.20	22.02	22.90	23.86	24.90	26.03	27.27					
88	28.64	30.14	31.82	33.69	35.80	38.19	40.92	44.07	47.74	52.08					
89	57.29	53.66	71.62	81.85	95.49	114.6	143.2	191.0	286.5	573.0					

Logarithmic Sines

Degrees	0′ 0.0°	6′ 0.1°	12′ 0.2°	18′ 0.3°	24′ 0.4°	30′ 0.5°	36′ 0.6°	42′ 0.7°	48′ 0.8°	54′ 0.9°	Mean Differences 1′	2′	3′	4′	5′
0°	$-\infty$	$\bar{3}.2419$	$\bar{3}.5429$	7190	8439	9408	$\bar{2}.0200$	$\bar{2}.0870$	$\bar{2}.1450$	$\bar{2}.1961$					
1	$\bar{2}.2419$	2832	3210	3558	3880	4179	4459	4723	4971	5206					
2	$\bar{2}.5428$	5640	5842	6035	6220	6397	6567	6731	6889	7041					
3	$\bar{2}.7188$	7330	7468	7602	7731	7857	7979	8098	8213	8326					
4	$\bar{2}.8436$	8543	8647	8749	8849	8946	9042	9135	9226	9315	16	32	48	64	80
5	$\bar{2}.9403$	9489	9573	9655	9736	9816	9894	9970	$\bar{1}.0046$	$\bar{1}.0120$	13	26	39	52	65
6	$\bar{1}.0192$	0264	0334	0403	0472	0539	0605	0670	0743	0797	11	22	33	44	55
7	$\bar{1}.0859$	0920	0981	1040	1099	1157	1214	1271	1326	1381	10	19	29	38	48
8	$\bar{1}.1436$	1489	1542	1594	1646	1697	1747	1797	1847	1895	8	17	25	34	42
9	$\bar{1}.1943$	1991	2038	2085	2131	2176	2221	2266	2310	2353	8	15	23	30	38
10°	$\bar{1}.2397$	2439	2482	2524	2565	2606	2647	2687	2727	2767	7	14	20	27	34
11	$\bar{1}.2806$	2845	2883	2921	2959	2997	3034	3070	3107	3143	6	12	19	25	31
12	$\bar{1}.3179$	3214	3250	3284	3319	3353	3387	3421	3455	3488	6	11	17	23	28
13	$\bar{1}.3521$	3554	3586	3618	3650	3682	3713	3745	3775	3806	5	11	16	21	26
14	$\bar{1}.3837$	3867	3897	3927	3957	3986	4015	4044	4073	4102	5	10	15	20	24
15	$\bar{1}.4130$	4158	4186	4214	4242	4269	4296	4323	4350	4377	5	9	14	18	23
16	$\bar{1}.4403$	4430	4456	4482	4508	4533	4559	4584	4609	4634	4	9	13	17	21
17	$\bar{1}.4659$	4684	4709	4733	4757	4781	4805	4829	4853	4876	4	8	12	16	20
18	$\bar{1}.4900$	4923	4946	4969	4992	5015	5037	5060	5082	5104	4	8	11	15	19
19	$\bar{1}.5126$	5148	5170	5192	5213	5235	5256	5278	5299	5320	4	7	11	14	18
20°	$\bar{1}.5341$	5361	5382	5402	5423	5443	5463	5484	5504	5523	3	7	10	14	17
21	$\bar{1}.5543$	5563	5583	5602	5621	5641	5660	5679	5698	5717	3	6	10	13	16
22	$\bar{1}.5736$	5754	5773	5792	5810	5828	5847	5865	5883	5901	3	6	9	12	15
23	$\bar{1}.5919$	5937	5954	5972	5990	6007	6024	6042	6059	6076	3	6	9	12	15
24	$\bar{1}.6093$	6110	6127	6144	6161	6177	6194	6210	6227	6243	3	6	8	11	14
25	$\bar{1}.6259$	6276	6292	6308	6324	6340	6356	6371	6387	6403	3	5	8	11	13
26	$\bar{1}.6418$	6434	6449	6465	6480	6495	6510	6526	6541	6556	3	5	8	10	13
27	$\bar{1}.6570$	6585	6600	6615	6629	6644	6659	6673	6687	6702	2	5	7	10	12
28	$\bar{1}.6716$	6730	6744	6759	6773	6787	6801	6814	6828	6842	2	5	7	9	12
29	$\bar{1}.6856$	6869	6883	6896	6910	6923	6937	6950	6963	6977	2	4	7	9	11
30°	$\bar{1}.6990$	7003	7016	7029	7042	7055	7068	7080	7093	7106	2	4	6	9	11
31	$\bar{1}.7118$	7131	7144	7156	7168	7181	7193	7205	7218	7230	2	4	6	8	10
32	$\bar{1}.7242$	7254	7266	7278	7290	7302	7314	7326	7338	7349	2	4	6	8	10
33	$\bar{1}.7361$	7373	7384	7396	7407	7419	7430	7442	7453	7464	2	4	6	8	10
34	$\bar{1}.7476$	7487	7498	7509	7520	7531	7542	7553	7564	7575	2	4	6	7	9
35	$\bar{1}.7586$	7597	7607	7618	7629	7640	7650	7661	7671	7682	2	4	5	7	9
36	$\bar{1}.7692$	7703	7713	7723	7734	7744	7754	7764	7774	7785	2	3	5	7	9
37	$\bar{1}.7795$	7805	7815	7825	7835	7844	7854	7864	7874	7884	2	3	5	7	8
38	$\bar{1}.7893$	7903	7913	7922	7932	7941	7951	7960	7970	7979	2	3	5	6	8
39	$\bar{1}.7989$	7998	8007	8017	8026	8035	8044	8053	8063	8072	2	3	5	6	8
40°	$\bar{1}.8081$	8090	8099	8108	8117	8125	8134	8143	8152	8161	1	3	4	6	7
41	$\bar{1}.8169$	8178	8187	8195	8204	8213	8221	8230	8238	8247	1	3	4	6	7
42	$\bar{1}.8255$	8264	8272	8280	8289	8297	8305	8313	8322	8330	1	3	4	6	7
43	$\bar{1}.8338$	8346	8354	8362	8370	8378	8386	8394	8402	8410	1	3	4	5	7
44	$\bar{1}.8418$	8426	8433	8441	8449	8457	8464	8472	8480	8487	1	3	4	5	6

Logarithmic Sines

Degrees	0′ 0.0°	6′ 0.1°	12′ 0.2°	18′ 0.3°	24′ 0.4°	30′ 0.5°	36′ 0.6°	42′ 0.7°	48′ 0.8°	54′ 0.9°	Mean Differences 1′	2′	3′	4′	5′
45°	$\bar{1}$.8495	8502	8510	8517	8525	8532	8540	8547	8555	8562	1	2	4	5	6
46	$\bar{1}$.8569	8577	8584	8591	8598	8606	8613	8620	8627	8634	1	2	4	5	6
47	$\bar{1}$.8641	8648	8655	8662	8669	8676	8683	8690	8697	8704	1	2	3	5	6
48	$\bar{1}$.8711	8718	8724	8731	8738	8745	8751	8758	8765	8771	1	2	3	4	6
49	$\bar{1}$.8778	8784	8791	8797	8804	8810	8817	8823	8830	8836	1	2	3	4	5
50°	$\bar{1}$.8843	8849	8855	8862	8868	8874	8880	8887	8893	8899	1	2	3	4	5
51	$\bar{1}$.8905	8911	8917	8923	8929	8935	8941	8947	8953	8959	1	2	3	4	5
52	$\bar{1}$.8965	8971	8977	8983	8989	8995	9000	9006	9012	9018	1	2	3	4	5
53	$\bar{1}$.9023	9029	9035	9041	9046	9052	9057	9063	9069	9074	1	2	3	4	5
54	$\bar{1}$.9080	9085	9091	9096	9101	9107	9112	9118	9123	9128	1	2	3	4	5
55	$\bar{1}$.9134	9139	9144	9149	9155	9160	9165	9170	9175	9181	1	2	3	3	4
56	$\bar{1}$.9186	9191	9196	9201	9206	9211	9216	9221	9226	9231	1	2	3	3	4
57	$\bar{1}$.9236	9241	9246	9251	9255	9260	9265	9270	9275	9279	1	2	2	3	4
58	$\bar{1}$.9284	9289	9294	9298	9303	9308	9312	9317	9322	9326	1	2	2	3	4
59	$\bar{1}$.9331	9335	9340	9344	9349	9353	9358	9362	9367	9371	1	1	2	3	4
60°	$\bar{1}$.9375	9380	9384	9388	9393	9397	9401	9406	9410	9414	1	1	2	3	4
61	$\bar{1}$.9418	9422	9427	9431	9435	9439	9443	9447	9451	9455	1	1	2	3	3
62	$\bar{1}$.9459	9463	9467	9471	9475	9479	9483	9487	9491	9495	1	1	2	3	3
63	$\bar{1}$.9499	9503	9507	9510	9514	9518	9522	9525	9529	9533	1	1	2	3	3
64	$\bar{1}$.9537	9540	9544	9548	9551	9555	9558	9562	9566	9569	1	1	2	2	3
65	$\bar{1}$.9573	9576	9580	9583	9587	9590	9594	9597	9601	9604	1	1	2	2	3
66	$\bar{1}$.9607	9611	9614	9617	9621	9624	9627	9631	9634	9637	1	1	2	2	3
67	$\bar{1}$.9640	9643	9647	9650	9653	9656	9659	9662	9666	9669	1	1	2	2	3
68	$\bar{1}$.9672	9675	9678	9681	9684	9687	9690	9693	9696	9699	0	1	1	2	2
69	$\bar{1}$.9702	9704	9707	9710	9713	9716	9719	9722	9724	9727	0	1	1	2	2
70°	$\bar{1}$.9730	9733	9735	9738	9741	9743	9746	9749	9751	9754	0	1	1	2	2
71	$\bar{1}$.9757	9759	9762	9764	9767	9770	9772	9775	9777	9780	0	1	1	2	2
72	$\bar{1}$.9782	9785	9787	9789	9792	9794	9797	9799	9801	9804	0	1	1	2	2
73	$\bar{1}$.9806	9808	9811	9813	9815	9817	9820	9822	9824	9826	0	1	1	2	2
74	$\bar{1}$.9828	9831	9833	9835	9837	9839	9841	9843	9845	9847	0	1	1	1	2
75	$\bar{1}$.9849	9851	9853	9855	9857	9859	9861	9863	9865	9867	0	1	1	1	2
76	$\bar{1}$.9869	9871	9873	9875	9876	9878	9880	9882	9884	9885	0	1	1	1	2
77	$\bar{1}$.9887	9889	9891	9892	9894	9896	9897	9899	9901	9902	0	1	1	1	1
78	$\bar{1}$.9904	9906	9907	9909	9910	9912	9913	9915	9916	9918	0	1	1	1	1
79	$\bar{1}$.9919	9921	9922	9924	9925	9927	9928	9929	9931	9932	0	0	1	1	1
80°	$\bar{1}$.9934	9935	9936	9937	9939	9940	9941	9943	9944	9945	0	0	1	1	1
81	$\bar{1}$.9946	9947	9949	9950	9951	9952	9953	9954	9955	9956	0	0	1	1	1
82	$\bar{1}$.9958	9959	9960	9961	9962	9963	9964	9965	9966	9967	0	0	1	1	1
83	$\bar{1}$.9968	9968	9969	9970	9971	9972	9973	9974	9975	9975	0	0	0	1	1
84	$\bar{1}$.9976	9977	9978	9978	9979	9980	9981	9981	9982	9983	0	0	0	0	1
85	$\bar{1}$.9983	9984	9985	9985	9986	9987	9987	9988	9988	9989	0	0	0	0	0
86	$\bar{1}$.9989	9990	9990	9991	9991	9992	9992	9993	9993	9994	0	0	0	0	0
87	$\bar{1}$.9994	9994	9995	9995	9996	9996	9996	9996	9997	9997	0	0	0	0	0
88	$\bar{1}$.9997	9998	9998	9998	9998	9999	9999	9999	9999	9999	0	0	0	0	0
89	$\bar{1}$.9999	9999	0.0000	0000	0000	0000	0000	0000	0000	0000	0	0	0	0	0

Logarithmic Cosines

[*N.B. – Subtract* Mean Differences]

Degrees	0′ 0.0°	6′ 0.1°	12′ 0.2°	18′ 0.3°	24′ 0.4°	30′ 0.5°	36′ 0.6°	42′ 0.7°	48′ 0.8°	54′ 0.9°	Mean Differences SUBTRACT 1′	2′	3′	4′	5′
0°	0.0000	0000	0000	0000	0000	0000	0000	0000	0000	$\bar{1}.9999$	0	0	0	0	0
1	$\bar{1}.9999$	9999	9999	9999	9999	9999	9998	9998	9998	9998	0	0	0	0	0
2	$\bar{1}.9997$	9997	9997	9996	9996	9996	9996	9995	9995	9994	0	0	0	0	0
3	$\bar{1}.9994$	9994	9993	9993	9992	9992	9991	9991	9990	9990	0	0	0	0	0
4	$\bar{1}.9989$	9989	9988	9988	9987	9987	9986	9985	9985	9984	0	0	0	0	0
5	$\bar{1}.9983$	9983	9982	9981	9981	9980	9979	9978	9978	9977	0	0	0	0	1
6	$\bar{1}.9976$	9975	9975	9974	9973	9972	9971	9970	9969	9968	0	0	0	1	1
7	$\bar{1}.9968$	9967	9966	9965	9964	9963	9962	9961	9960	9959	0	0	1	1	1
8	$\bar{1}.9958$	9956	9955	9954	9953	9952	9951	9950	9949	9947	0	0	1	1	1
9	$\bar{1}.9946$	9945	9944	9943	9941	9940	9939	9937	9936	9935	0	0	1	1	1
10°	$\bar{1}.9934$	9932	9931	9929	9928	9927	9925	9924	9922	9921	0	0	1	1	1
11	$\bar{1}.9919$	9918	9916	9915	9913	9912	9910	9909	9907	9906	0	1	1	1	1
12	$\bar{1}.9904$	9902	9901	9899	9897	9896	9894	9892	9891	9889	0	1	1	1	1
13	$\bar{1}.9887$	9885	9884	9882	9880	9878	9876	9875	9873	9871	0	1	1	1	2
14	$\bar{1}.9869$	9867	9865	9863	9861	9859	9857	9855	9853	9851	0	1	1	1	2
15	$\bar{1}.9849$	9847	9845	9843	9841	9839	9837	9835	9833	9831	0	1	1	1	2
16	$\bar{1}.9828$	9826	9824	9822	9820	9817	9815	9813	9811	9808	0	1	1	2	2
17	$\bar{1}.9806$	9804	9801	9799	9797	9794	9792	9789	9787	9785	0	1	1	2	2
18	$\bar{1}.9782$	9780	9777	9775	9772	9770	9767	9764	9762	9759	0	1	1	2	2
19	$\bar{1}.9757$	9754	9751	9749	9746	9743	9741	9738	9735	9733	0	1	1	2	2
20°	$\bar{1}.9730$	9727	9724	9722	9719	9716	9713	9710	9707	9704	0	1	1	2	2
21	$\bar{1}.9702$	9699	9696	9693	9690	9687	9684	9681	9678	9675	0	1	1	2	2
22	$\bar{1}.9672$	9669	9666	9662	9659	9656	9653	9650	9647	9643	1	1	2	2	3
23	$\bar{1}.9640$	9637	9634	9631	9627	9624	9621	9617	9614	9611	1	1	2	2	3
24	$\bar{1}.9607$	9604	9601	9597	9594	9590	9587	9583	9580	9576	1	1	2	2	3
25	$\bar{1}.9573$	9569	9566	9562	9558	9555	9551	9548	9544	9540	1	1	2	2	3
26	$\bar{1}.9537$	9533	9529	9525	9522	9518	9514	9510	9506	9503	1	1	2	3	3
27	$\bar{1}.9499$	9495	9491	9487	9483	9479	9475	9471	9467	9463	1	1	2	3	3
28	$\bar{1}.9459$	9455	9451	9447	9443	9439	9435	9431	9427	9422	1	1	2	3	3
29	$\bar{1}.9418$	9414	9410	9406	9401	9397	9393	9388	9384	9380	1	1	2	3	4
30°	$\bar{1}.9375$	9371	9367	9362	9358	9353	9349	9344	9340	9335	1	1	2	3	4
31	$\bar{1}.9331$	9326	9322	9317	9312	9308	9303	9298	9294	9289	1	2	2	3	4
32	$\bar{1}.9284$	9279	9275	9270	9265	9260	9255	9251	9246	9241	1	2	2	3	4
33	$\bar{1}.9236$	9231	9226	9221	9216	9211	9206	9201	9196	9191	1	2	3	3	4
34	$\bar{1}.9186$	9181	9175	9170	9165	9160	9155	9149	9144	9139	1	2	3	3	4
35	$\bar{1}.9134$	9128	9123	9118	9112	9107	9101	9096	9091	9085	1	2	3	4	5
36	$\bar{1}.9080$	9074	9069	9063	9057	9052	9046	9041	9035	9029	1	2	3	4	5
37	$\bar{1}.9023$	9018	9012	9006	9000	8995	8989	8983	8977	8971	1	2	3	4	5
38	$\bar{1}.8965$	8959	8953	8947	8941	8935	8929	8923	8917	8911	1	2	3	4	5
39	$\bar{1}.8905$	8899	8893	8887	8880	8874	8868	8862	8855	8849	1	2	3	4	5
40°	$\bar{1}.8843$	8836	8830	8823	8817	8810	8804	8797	8791	8784	1	2	3	4	5
41	$\bar{1}.8778$	8771	8765	8758	8751	8745	8738	8731	8724	8718	1	2	3	5	6
42	$\bar{1}.8711$	8704	8697	8690	8683	8676	8669	8662	8655	8648	1	2	3	5	6
43	$\bar{1}.8641$	8634	8627	8620	8613	8606	8598	8591	8584	8577	1	2	4	5	6
44	$\bar{1}.8569$	8562	8555	8547	8540	8532	8525	8517	8510	8502	1	2	4	5	6

Logarithmic Cosines

[*N.B. – Subtract* Mean Differences]

Degrees	0′ 0.0°	6′ 0.1°	12′ 0.2°	18′ 0.3°	24′ 0.4°	30′ 0.5°	36′ 0.6°	42′ 0.7°	48′ 0.8°	54′ 0.9°	Mean Differences SUBTRACT 1′	2′	3′	4′	5′
45°	$\bar{1}$.8495	8487	8480	8472	8464	8457	8449	8441	8433	8426	1	3	4	5	6
46	$\bar{1}$.8418	8410	8402	8394	8386	8378	8370	8362	8354	8346	1	3	4	5	7
47	$\bar{1}$.8338	8330	8322	8313	8305	8297	8289	8280	8272	8264	1	3	4	6	7
48	$\bar{1}$.8255	8247	8238	8230	8221	8213	8204	8195	8187	8178	1	3	4	6	7
49	$\bar{1}$.8169	8161	8152	8143	8134	8125	8117	8108	8099	8090	1	3	4	6	7
50°	$\bar{1}$.8081	8072	8063	8053	8044	8035	8026	8017	8007	7998	2	3	5	6	8
51	$\bar{1}$.7989	7979	7970	7960	7951	7941	7932	7922	7913	7903	2	3	5	6	8
52	$\bar{1}$.7893	7884	7874	7864	7854	7844	7835	7825	7815	7805	2	3	5	7	8
53	$\bar{1}$.7795	7785	7774	7764	7754	7744	7734	7723	7713	7703	2	3	5	7	9
54	$\bar{1}$.7692	7682	7671	7661	7650	7640	7629	7618	7607	7597	2	4	5	7	9
55	$\bar{1}$.7586	7575	7564	7553	7542	7531	7520	7509	7498	7487	2	4	6	7	9
56	$\bar{1}$.7476	7464	7453	7442	7430	7419	7407	7396	7384	7373	2	4	6	8	10
57	$\bar{1}$.7361	7349	7338	7326	7314	7302	7290	7278	7266	7254	2	4	6	8	10
58	$\bar{1}$.7242	7230	7218	7205	7193	7181	7168	7156	7144	7131	2	4	7	8	10
59	$\bar{1}$.7118	7106	7093	7080	7068	7055	7042	7029	7016	7003	2	4	6	9	11
60°	$\bar{1}$.6990	6977	6963	6950	6937	6923	6910	6896	6883	6869	2	4	7	9	11
61	$\bar{1}$.6856	6842	6828	6814	6801	6787	6773	6759	6744	6730	2	5	7	9	12
62	$\bar{1}$.6716	6702	6687	6673	6659	6644	6629	6615	6600	6585	2	5	7	10	12
63	$\bar{1}$.6570	6556	6541	6526	6510	6495	6480	6465	6449	6434	3	5	8	10	13
64	$\bar{1}$.6418	6403	6387	6371	6356	6340	6324	6308	6292	6276	3	5	8	11	13
65	$\bar{1}$.6259	6243	6227	6210	6194	6177	6161	6144	6127	6110	3	6	8	11	14
66	$\bar{1}$.6093	6076	6059	6042	6024	6007	5990	5972	5954	5937	3	6	9	12	15
67	$\bar{1}$.5919	5901	5883	5865	5847	5828	5810	5792	5773	5754	3	6	9	12	15
68	$\bar{1}$.5736	5717	5698	5679	5660	5641	5621	5602	5583	5563	3	6	10	13	16
69°	$\bar{1}$.5543	5523	5504	5484	5463	5443	5423	5402	5382	5361	3	7	10	14	17
70°	$\bar{1}$.5341	5320	5299	5278	5256	5235	5213	5192	5170	5148	4	7	11	14	18
71	$\bar{1}$.5126	5104	5082	5060	5037	5015	4992	4969	4946	4923	4	8	11	15	19
72	$\bar{1}$.4900	4876	4853	4829	4805	4781	4757	4733	4709	4684	4	8	12	16	20
73	$\bar{1}$.4659	4634	4609	4584	4559	4533	4508	4482	4456	4430	4	9	13	17	21
74	$\bar{1}$.4403	4377	4350	4323	4296	4269	4242	4214	4186	4158	5	9	14	18	23
75	$\bar{1}$.4130	4102	4073	4044	4015	3986	3957	3927	3897	3867	5	10	15	20	24
76	$\bar{1}$.3837	3806	3775	3745	3713	3682	3650	3618	3586	3554	5	11	16	21	26
77	$\bar{1}$.3521	3488	3455	3421	3387	3353	3319	3284	3250	3214	6	11	17	23	28
78	$\bar{1}$.3179	3143	3107	3070	3034	2997	2959	2921	2883	2845	6	12	19	25	31
79	$\bar{1}$.2806	2767	2727	2687	2647	2606	2565	2524	2482	2439	7	14	20	27	34
80°	$\bar{1}$.2397	2353	2310	2266	2221	2176	2131	2085	2038	1991	8	15	23	30	38
81	$\bar{1}$.1943	1895	1847	1797	1747	1697	1646	1594	1524	1489	8	17	25	34	42
82	$\bar{1}$.1436	1381	1326	1271	1214	1157	1099	1040	0981	0920	10	19	29	38	48
83	$\bar{1}$.0859	0797	0734	0670	0605	0539	0472	0403	0334	0254	11	22	33	44	55
84	$\bar{1}$.0192	0120	0046	$\bar{2}$.9970	$\bar{2}$.9894	$\bar{2}$.9816	$\bar{2}$.9736	$\bar{2}$.9655	$\bar{2}$.9573	$\bar{2}$.9489	13	26	39	52	65
85°	$\bar{2}$.9403	9315	9226	9135	9042	8946	8849	8749	8647	8543	16	32	48	64	80
86	$\bar{2}$.8436	8326	8213	8098	7979	7857	7731	7602	7468	7330					
87	$\bar{2}$.7188	7041	6889	6731	6567	6397	6220	6035	5842	5640					
88	$\bar{2}$.5428	5206	4971	4723	4459	4179	3880	3558	3210	2832					
89	$\bar{2}$.2419	1961	1450	0870	0200	$\bar{3}$.9408	$\bar{3}$.8439	$\bar{3}$.7190	$\bar{3}$.5429	$\bar{3}$.2419					

Logarithmic Tangents

Degrees	0′ 0.0	6′ 0.1	12′ 0.2	18′ 0.3	24′ 0.4	30′ 0.5	36′ 0.6	42′ 0.7	48′ 0.8	54′ 0.9	Mean Differences 1	2	3	4	5
0		$\bar{3}.2419$	$\bar{3}.5429$	$\bar{3}.7190$	$\bar{3}.8439$	$\bar{3}.9409$	$\bar{2}.0200$	$\bar{2}.0870$	$\bar{2}.1450$	$\bar{2}.1962$					
1	$\bar{2}.2419$	2833	3211	3559	3881	4181	4461	4725	4973	5208					
2	$\bar{2}.5431$	5643	5845	6038	6223	6401	6571	6736	6894	7046					
3	$\bar{2}.7194$	7337	7475	7609	7739	7865	7988	8017	8223	8336					
4	$\bar{2}.8446$	8554	8659	8762	8862	8960	9056	9150	9241	9331	16	32	48	64	81
5	$\bar{2}.9420$	9506	9591	9674	9756	9836	9915	9992	$\bar{1}.0068$	$\bar{1}.0143$	13	26	40	53	66
6	$\bar{1}.0216$	0289	0360	0430	0499	0567	0633	0699	0764	0828	11	22	34	45	56
7	$\bar{1}.0891$	0954	1015	1076	1135	1194	1252	1310	1367	1423	10	20	29	39	49
8	$\bar{1}.1478$	1533	1587	1640	1693	1745	1797	1848	1898	1948	9	17	26	35	43
9	$\bar{1}.1997$	2046	2094	2142	2189	2236	2282	2328	2374	2419	8	16	23	31	39
10	$\bar{1}.2463$	2507	2551	2594	2637	2680	2722	2764	2805	2846	7	14	21	28	35
11	$\bar{1}.2887$	2927	2967	3006	3046	3085	3123	3162	3200	3237	6	13	19	26	32
12	$\bar{1}.3275$	3312	3349	3385	3422	3458	3493	3529	3564	3599	6	12	18	24	30
13	$\bar{1}.3634$	3668	3702	3736	3770	3804	3837	3870	3903	3935	6	11	17	22	28
14	$\bar{1}.3968$	0000	4032	4064	4095	4127	4158	4189	4220	4250	5	10	16	21	26
15	$\bar{1}.4281$	4311	4341	4371	4400	4430	4459	4488	4517	4546	5	10	15	20	25
16	$\bar{1}.4575$	4603	4632	4660	4688	4716	4744	4771	4799	4826	5	9	14	19	23
17	$\bar{1}.4853$	4880	4907	4934	4961	4987	5014	5040	5066	5092	4	9	13	18	22
18	$\bar{1}.5118$	5143	5169	5195	5220	5245	5270	5295	5320	5345	4	8	13	17	21
19	$\bar{1}.5370$	5394	5419	5443	5467	5491	5516	5539	5563	5587	4	8	12	16	20
20	$\bar{1}.5611$	5634	5658	5681	5704	5727	5750	5773	5796	5819	4	8	12	15	19
21	$\bar{1}.5842$	5864	5887	5909	5932	5954	5976	5998	6020	6042	4	7	11	15	19
22	$\bar{1}.6064$	6086	6108	6129	6151	6172	6194	6215	6236	6257	4	7	11	14	18
23	$\bar{1}.6279$	6300	6321	6341	6362	6383	6404	6424	6445	6465	3	7	10	14	17
24	$\bar{1}.6486$	6506	6527	6547	6567	6587	6607	6627	6647	6667	3	7	10	13	17
25	$\bar{1}.6687$	6706	6726	6746	6765	6785	6804	6824	6843	6863	3	7	10	13	16
26	$\bar{1}.6882$	6901	6920	6939	6958	6977	6996	7015	7034	7053	3	6	9	13	16
27	$\bar{1}.7072$	7090	7109	7128	7146	7165	7183	7202	7220	7238	3	6	9	12	15
28	$\bar{1}.7257$	7275	7293	7311	7330	7348	7366	7384	7402	7420	3	6	9	12	15
29	$\bar{1}.7438$	7455	7473	7491	7509	7526	7544	7562	7579	7597	3	6	9	12	15
30	$\bar{1}.7614$	7632	7649	7667	7684	7701	7719	7736	7753	7771	3	6	9	12	14
31	$\bar{1}.7788$	7805	7822	7839	7856	7873	7890	7907	7924	7941	3	6	9	11	14
32	$\bar{1}.7958$	7975	7992	8008	8025	8042	8059	8075	8092	8109	3	6	8	11	14
33	$\bar{1}.8125$	8142	8158	8175	8191	8208	8224	8241	8257	8274	3	5	8	11	14
34	$\bar{1}.8290$	8306	8323	8339	8355	8371	8388	8404	8420	8436	3	5	8	11	14
35	$\bar{1}.8452$	8468	8484	8501	8517	8533	8549	8565	8581	8597	3	5	8	11	13
36	$\bar{1}.8613$	8629	8644	8660	8676	8692	8708	8724	8740	8755	3	5	8	11	13
37	$\bar{1}.8771$	8787	8803	8818	8834	8850	8865	8881	8897	8912	3	5	8	10	13
38	$\bar{1}.8928$	8944	8959	8975	8990	9006	9022	9037	9053	9068	3	5	8	10	13
39	$\bar{1}.9084$	9099	9115	9130	9146	9161	9176	9192	9207	9223	3	5	8	10	13
40	$\bar{1}.9238$	9254	9269	9284	9300	9315	9330	9346	9361	9376	3	5	8	10	13
41	$\bar{1}.9392$	9407	9422	9438	9453	9468	9483	9499	9514	9529	3	5	8	10	13
42	$\bar{1}.9544$	9560	9575	9590	9605	9621	9636	9651	9666	9681	3	5	8	10	13
43	$\bar{1}.9697$	9712	9727	9742	9757	9772	9788	9803	9818	9833	3	5	8	10	13
44	$\bar{1}.9848$	9864	9879	9894	9909	9924	9939	9955	9970	9985	3	5	8	10	13

Logarithmic Tangents

Degrees	0′ 0.0°	6′ 0.1°	12′ 0.2°	18′ 0.3°	24′ 0.4°	30′ 0.5°	36′ 0.6°	42′ 0.7°	48′ 0.8°	54′ 0.9°	Mean Differences 1′	2′	3′	4′	5′
45°	0.0000	0015	0030	0045	0061	0076	0091	0106	0121	0136	3	5	8	10	13
46	0.0152	0167	0182	0197	0212	0228	0243	0258	0273	0288	3	5	8	10	13
47	0.0303	0319	0334	0349	0364	0379	0395	0410	0425	0440	3	5	8	10	13
48	0.0456	0471	0486	0501	0517	0532	0547	0562	0578	0593	3	5	8	10	13
49	0.0608	0624	0639	0654	0670	0685	0700	0716	0731	0746	3	5	8	10	13
50°	0.0762	0777	0793	0808	0824	0839	0854	0870	0885	0901	3	5	8	10	13
51	0.0916	0932	0947	0963	0978	0994	1010	1025	1041	1056	3	5	8	10	13
52	0.1072	1088	1103	1119	1135	1150	1166	1182	1197	1213	3	5	8	10	13
53	0.1229	1245	1260	1276	1292	1308	1324	1340	1356	1371	3	5	8	11	13
54	0.1387	1403	1419	1435	1451	1467	1483	1499	1516	1532	3	5	8	11	13
55	0.1548	1564	1580	1596	1612	1629	1645	1661	1677	1694	4	5	8	11	14
56	0.1710	1726	1743	1759	1776	1792	1809	1825	1842	1858	3	5	8	11	14
57	0.1875	1891	1908	1925	1941	1958	1975	1992	2008	2025	3	6	8	11	14
58	0.2042	2059	2076	2093	2110	2127	2144	2161	2178	2195	3	6	9	11	14
59	0.2212	2229	2247	2264	2281	2299	2316	2333	2351	2368	3	6	9	12	14
60°	0.2386	2403	2421	2438	2456	2474	2491	2509	2527	2545	3	6	9	12	15
61	0.2562	2580	2598	2616	2634	2652	2670	2689	2707	2725	3	6	9	12	15
62	0.2743	2762	2780	2798	2817	2835	2854	2872	2891	2910	3	6	9	12	15
63	0.2928	2947	2966	2985	3004	3023	3042	3061	3080	3099	3	6	9	13	16
64	0.3118	3137	3157	3176	3196	3215	3235	3254	3274	3294	3	6	10	13	16
65	0.3313	3333	3353	3373	3393	3413	3433	3453	3473	3494	3	7	10	13	17
66	0.3514	3535	3555	3576	3596	3617	3638	3659	3679	3700	3	7	10	14	17
67	0.3721	3743	3764	3785	3806	3828	3849	3871	3892	3914	4	7	11	14	18
68	0.3936	3958	3980	4002	4024	4046	4068	4091	4113	4136	4	7	11	15	19
69	0.4158	4181	4204	4227	4250	4273	4296	4319	4342	4366	4	8	12	15	19
70°	0.4389	4413	4437	4461	4484	4509	4533	4557	4581	4606	4	8	12	16	20
71	0.4630	4655	4680	4705	4730	4755	4780	4805	4831	4857	4	8	13	17	21
72	0.4882	4908	4934	4960	4986	5013	5039	5066	5093	5120	4	9	13	18	22
73	0.5147	5174	5201	5229	5256	5284	5312	5340	5368	5397	5	9	14	19	23
74	0.5425	5454	5483	5512	5541	5570	5600	5629	5659	5689	5	10	15	20	25
75	0.5719	5750	5780	5811	5842	5873	5905	5936	5968	6000	5	10	16	21	26
76	0.6032	6065	6097	6130	6163	6196	6230	6264	6298	6332	6	11	17	22	28
77	0.6366	6401	6436	6471	6507	6542	6578	6615	6651	6688	6	12	18	24	30
78	0.6725	6763	6800	6838	6877	6915	6954	6994	7033	7073	6	13	19	26	32
79	0.7113	7154	7195	7236	7278	7320	7363	7406	7449	7493	7	14	21	28	35
80°	0.7537	7581	7626	7672	7718	7764	7811	7858	7906	7954	8	16	23	31	39
81	0.8003	8052	8102	8152	8203	8255	8307	8360	8413	8467	9	17	26	35	43
82	0.8522	8577	8632	8690	8748	8806	8865	8924	8985	9046	10	20	29	39	49
83	0.9109	9172	9236	9301	9367	9433	9501	9570	9640	9711	11	22	34	45	56
84	0.9784	9857	9932	1.0008	1.0085	1.0164	1.0244	1.0326	1.0409	1.0494	13	26	40	53	66
85	1.0580	0669	0759	0850	0944	1040	1138	1238	1341	1446	16	32	48	64	81
86	1.1554	1664	1777	1893	2012	2135	2261	2391	2525	2663					
87	1.2806	2954	3106	3264	3429	3599	3777	3962	4155	4357					
88	1.4569	4792	5027	5275	5539	5819	6119	6441	6789	7167					
89	1.7581	8038	8550	9130	9800	2.0591	2.1561	2.2810	2.4571	2.7581					

Reciprocals of Four-Figure Numbers

	0	1	2	3	4	5	6	7	8	9	Mean Differences SUBTRACT								
											1	2	3	4	5	6	7	8	9
1.0	1.0000	9901	9804	9709	9615	9524	9434	9346	9259	9174	9	18	28	37	46	55	64	74	83
1.1	.9091	9009	8929	8850	8772	8696	8621	8547	8475	8403	8	15	23	31	38	46	53	61	69
1.2	.8333	8264	8197	8130	8065	8000	7937	7874	7813	7752	7	13	20	26	33	39	46	52	59
1.3	.7692	7634	7576	7519	7463	7407	7353	7299	7246	7194	6	11	17	22	28	33	39	44	50
1.4	.7143	7092	7042	6993	6944	6897	6849	6803	6757	6711	5	10	14	19	24	29	33	38	43
1.5	.6667	6623	6579	6536	6494	6452	6410	6369	6329	6289	4	8	13	17	21	25	29	33	38
1.6	.6250	6211	6173	6135	6098	6061	6024	5988	5952	5917	4	7	11	15	18	22	26	29	33
1.7	.5882	5848	5814	5780	5747	5714	5682	5650	5618	5587	3	7	10	13	16	20	23	26	29
1.8	.5556	5525	5495	5464	5435	5405	5376	5348	5319	5291	3	6	9	12	15	17	20	23	26
1.9	.5263	5236	5208	5181	5155	5128	5102	5076	5051	5025	3	5	8	11	13	16	18	21	24
2.0	.5000	4975	4950	4926	4902	4878	4854	4831	4808	4785	2	5	7	10	12	14	17	19	21
2.1	.4762	4739	4717	4695	4673	4651	4630	4698	4587	4566	2	4	7	9	11	13	15	17	19
2.2	.4545	4525	4505	4484	4464	4444	4425	4405	4386	4367	2	4	6	8	10	12	14	16	18
2.3	.4348	4329	4310	4292	4274	4255	4237	4219	4202	4184	2	4	5	7	9	11	13	14	16
2.4	.4167	4149	4132	4115	4098	4082	4065	4049	4032	4016	2	3	5	7	8	10	12	13	15
2.5	.4000	3984	3968	3953	3937	3922	3906	3891	3876	3861	2	3	5	6	8	9	11	12	14
2.6	.3846	3831	3817	3802	3788	3774	3759	3745	3731	3717	1	3	4	6	7	9	10	11	13
2.7	.3704	3690	3676	3663	3650	3636	3623	3610	3597	3584	1	3	4	5	7	8	9	11	12
2.8	.3571	3559	3546	3534	3521	3509	3497	3484	3472	3460	1	2	4	5	6	7	9	10	11
2.9	.3448	3436	3425	3413	3401	3390	3378	3367	3356	3344	1	2	3	5	6	7	8	9	10
3.0	.3333	3322	3311	3300	3289	3279	3268	3257	3247	3236	1	2	3	4	5	6	7	9	10
3.1	.3226	3215	3205	3195	3185	3175	3165	3155	3145	3135	1	2	3	4	5	6	7	8	9
3.2	.3125	3115	3106	3096	3086	3077	3067	3058	3049	3040	1	2	3	4	5	6	7	8	9
3.3	.3030	3021	3012	3003	2994	2985	2976	2967	2959	2950	1	2	3	4	4	5	6	7	8
3.4	.2941	2933	2924	2915	2907	2899	2890	2882	2874	2865	1	2	3	3	4	5	6	7	8
3.5	.2857	2849	2841	2833	2825	2817	2809	2801	2793	2786	1	2	2	3	4	5	6	6	7
3.6	.2778	2770	2762	2755	2747	2740	2732	2725	2717	2710	1	2	2	3	4	5	5	6	7
3.7	.2703	2695	2688	2681	2674	2667	2660	2653	2646	2639	1	1	2	3	4	4	5	6	6
3.8	.2632	2625	2618	2611	2604	2597	2591	2584	2577	2571	1	1	2	3	3	4	5	5	6
3.9	.2564	2558	2551	2545	2538	2532	2525	2519	2513	2506	1	1	2	3	3	4	4	5	6
4.0	.2500	2494	2488	2481	2475	2469	2463	2457	2451	2445	1	1	2	2	3	4	4	5	5
4.1	.2439	2433	2427	2421	2415	2410	2404	2398	2392	2387	1	1	2	2	3	3	4	5	5
4.2	.2381	2375	2370	2364	2358	2353	2347	2342	2336	2331	1	1	2	2	3	3	4	4	5
4.3	.2326	2320	2315	2309	2304	2299	2294	2288	2283	2278	1	1	2	2	3	3	4	4	5
4.4	.2273	2268	2262	2257	2252	2247	2242	2237	2232	2227	1	1	2	2	3	3	4	4	5
4.5	.2222	2217	2212	2208	2203	2198	2193	2188	2183	2179	0	1	1	2	2	3	3	4	4
4.6	.2174	2169	2165	2160	2155	2151	2146	2141	2137	2132	0	1	1	2	2	3	3	4	4
4.7	.2128	2123	2119	2114	2110	2105	2101	2096	2092	2088	0	1	1	2	2	3	3	4	4
4.8	.2083	2079	2075	2070	2066	2062	2058	2053	2049	2045	0	1	1	2	2	3	3	3	4
4.9	.2041	2037	2033	2028	2024	2020	2016	2012	2008	2004	0	1	1	2	2	2	3	3	4
5.0	.2000	1996	1992	1988	1984	1980	1976	1972	1969	1965	0	1	1	2	2	2	3	3	4
5.1	.1961	1957	1953	1949	1946	1942	1938	1934	1931	1927	0	1	1	2	2	2	3	3	3
5.2	.1923	1919	1916	1912	1908	1905	1901	1898	1894	1890	0	1	1	1	2	2	3	3	3
5.3	.1887	1883	1880	1876	1873	1869	1866	1862	1859	1855	0	1	1	1	2	2	2	3	3
5.4	.1852	1848	1845	1842	1838	1835	1832	1828	1825	1821	0	1	1	1	2	2	2	3	3

$$\frac{1}{3.748} = 0.2674 - 0.0006 = 0.2668$$

$$\frac{1}{3748} = \frac{1}{10^3 \times 3.748} = 10^{-3} \times 0.2668 = 0.0002668$$

$$\frac{1}{0.03748} = \frac{1}{10^{-2} \times 3.748} = 10^2 \times 0.2668 = 26.68$$

Reciprocals of Four-Figure Numbers

	0	1	2	3	4	5	6	7	8	9	Mean Differences SUBTRACT 1	2	3	4	5	6	7	8	9
5.5	.1818	1815	1812	1808	1805	1802	1799	1795	1792	1789	0	1	1	1	2	2	2	3	3
5.6	.1786	1783	1779	1776	1773	1770	1767	1764	1761	1757	0	1	1	1	2	2	2	3	3
5.7	.1754	1751	1748	1745	1742	1739	1736	1733	1730	1727	0	1	1	1	1	2	2	2	3
5.8	.1724	1721	1718	1715	1712	1709	1706	1704	1701	1698	0	1	1	1	1	2	2	2	3
5.9	.1695	1692	1689	1686	1684	1681	1678	1675	1672	1669	0	1	1	1	1	2	2	2	3
6.0	.1667	1664	1661	1658	1656	1653	1650	1647	1645	1642	0	1	1	1	1	2	2	2	3
6.1	.1639	1637	1634	1631	1629	1626	1623	1621	1618	1616	0	1	1	1	1	2	2	2	2
6.2	.1613	1610	1608	1605	1603	1600	1597	1595	1592	1590	0	1	1	1	1	2	2	2	2
6.3	.1587	1585	1582	1580	1577	1575	1572	1570	1567	1565	0	0	1	1	1	1	2	2	2
6.4	.1562	1560	1558	1555	1553	1550	1548	1546	1543	1541	0	0	1	1	1	1	2	2	2
6.5	.1538	1536	1534	1531	1529	1527	1524	1522	1520	1517	0	0	1	1	1	1	2	2	2
6.6	.1515	1513	1511	1508	1506	1504	1502	1499	1497	1495	0	0	1	1	1	1	2	2	2
6.7	.1493	1490	1488	1486	1484	1481	1479	1477	1475	1473	0	0	1	1	1	1	2	2	2
6.8	.1471	1468	1466	1464	1462	1460	1458	1456	1453	1451	0	0	1	1	1	1	2	2	2
6.9	.1449	1447	1445	1443	1441	1439	1437	1435	1433	1431	0	0	1	1	1	1	2	2	2
7.0	.1429	1427	1425	1422	1420	1418	1416	1414	1412	1410	0	0	1	1	1	1	1	2	2
7.1	.1408	1406	1404	1403	1401	1399	1397	1395	1393	1391	0	0	1	1	1	1	1	2	2
7.2	.1389	1387	1385	1383	1381	1379	1377	1376	1374	1372	0	0	1	1	1	1	1	2	2
7.3	.1370	1368	1366	1364	1362	1361	1359	1357	1355	1353	0	0	1	1	1	1	1	2	2
7.4	.1351	1350	1348	1346	1344	1342	1340	1339	1337	1335	0	0	1	1	1	1	1	1	2
7.5	.1333	1332	1330	1328	1326	1325	1323	1321	1319	1318	0	0	1	1	1	1	1	1	2
7.6	.1316	1314	1312	1311	1309	1307	1305	1304	1302	1300	0	0	1	1	1	1	1	1	2
7.7	.1299	1297	1295	1294	1292	1290	1289	1287	1285	1284	0	0	0	1	1	1	1	1	1
7.8	.1282	1280	1279	1277	1276	1274	1272	1271	1269	1267	0	0	0	1	1	1	1	1	1
7.9	.1266	1264	1263	1261	1259	1258	1256	1255	1253	1252	0	0	0	1	1	1	1	1	1
8.0	.1250	1248	1247	1245	1244	1242	1241	1239	1238	1236	0	0	0	1	1	1	1	1	1
8.1	.1235	1233	1232	1230	1229	1227	1225	1224	1222	1221	0	0	0	1	1	1	1	1	1
8.2	.1220	1218	1217	1215	1214	1212	1211	1209	1208	1206	0	0	0	1	1	1	1	1	1
8.3	.1205	1203	1202	1200	1199	1198	1196	1195	1193	1192	0	0	0	1	1	1	1	1	1
8.4	.1190	1189	1188	1186	1185	1183	1182	1181	1179	1178	0	0	0	1	1	1	1	1	1
8.5	.1176	1175	1174	1172	1171	1170	1168	1167	1166	1164	0	0	0	1	1	1	1	1	1
8.6	.1163	1161	1160	1159	1157	1156	1155	1153	1152	1151	0	0	0	1	1	1	1	1	1
8.7	.1149	1148	1147	1145	1144	1143	1142	1140	1139	1138	0	0	0	1	1	1	1	1	1
8.8	.1136	1135	1134	1133	1131	1130	1129	1127	1126	1125	0	0	0	1	1	1	1	1	1
8.9	.1124	1122	1121	1120	1119	1117	1116	1115	1114	1112	0	0	0	1	1	1	1	1	1
9.0	.1111	1110	1109	1107	1106	1105	1104	1103	1101	1100	0	0	0	1	1	1	1	1	1
9.1	.1099	1098	1096	1095	1094	1093	1092	1090	1089	1088	0	0	0	0	1	1	1	1	1
9.2	.1087	1086	1085	1083	1082	1081	1080	1079	1078	1076	0	0	0	0	1	1	1	1	1
9.3	.1075	1074	1073	1072	1071	1070	1068	1067	1066	1065	0	0	0	0	1	1	1	1	1
9.4	.1064	1063	1062	1060	1059	1058	1057	1056	1055	1054	0	0	0	0	1	1	1	1	1
9.5	.1053	1052	1050	1049	1048	1047	1046	1045	1044	1043	0	0	0	0	1	1	1	1	1
9.6	.1042	1041	1039	1038	1037	1036	1035	1034	1033	1032	0	0	0	0	1	1	1	1	1
9.7	.1031	1030	1029	1028	1027	1026	1025	1024	1022	1021	0	0	0	0	1	1	1	1	1
9.8	.1020	1019	1018	1017	1016	1015	1014	1013	1012	1011	0	0	0	0	1	1	1	1	1
9.9	.1010	1009	1008	1007	1006	1005	1004	1003	1002	1001	0	0	0	0	0	1	1	1	1

Squares

	0	1	2	3	4	5	6	7	8	9
0	0	1	4	9	16	25	36	49	64	81
1	100	121	144	169	196	225	256	289	324	361
2	400	441	484	529	576	625	676	729	784	841
3	900	961	1024	1089	1156	1225	1296	1369	1444	1521
4	1600	1681	1764	1849	1936	2025	2116	2209	2304	2401
5	2500	2601	2704	2809	2916	3025	3136	3249	3364	3481
6	3600	3721	3844	3969	4096	4225	4356	4489	4624	4761
7	4900	5041	5184	5329	5476	5625	5776	5929	6084	6241
8	6400	6561	6724	6889	7056	7225	7396	7569	7744	7921
9	8100	8281	8464	8649	8836	9025	9216	9409	9604	9801
10	10000	10201	10404	10609	10816	11025	11236	11449	11664	11881
11	12100	12321	12544	12769	12996	13225	13456	13689	13924	14161
12	14400	14641	14884	15129	15376	15625	15876	16129	16384	16641
13	16900	17161	17424	17689	17956	18225	18496	18769	19044	19321
14	19600	19881	20164	20449	20736	21025	21316	21609	21904	22201
15	22500	22801	23104	23409	23716	24025	24336	24649	24964	25281
16	25600	25921	26244	26569	26896	27225	27556	27889	28224	28561
17	28900	29241	29584	29929	30276	30625	30976	31329	31684	32041
18	32400	32761	33124	33489	33856	34225	34596	34969	35344	35721
19	36100	36481	36864	37249	37636	38025	38416	38809	39204	39601
20	40000	40401	40804	41209	41616	42025	42436	42849	43264	43681
21	44100	44521	44944	45369	45796	46225	46656	47089	47524	47961
22	48400	48841	49284	49729	50176	50625	51076	51529	51984	52441
23	52900	53361	53824	54289	54756	55225	55696	56169	56644	57121
24	57600	58081	58564	59049	59536	60025	60516	61009	61504	62001
25	62500	63001	63504	64009	64516	65025	65536	66049	66564	67081
26	67600	68121	68644	69169	69696	70225	70756	71289	71824	72361
27	72900	73441	73984	74529	75076	75625	76176	76729	77284	77841
28	78400	78961	79524	80089	80656	81225	81796	82369	82944	83521
29	84100	84681	85264	85849	86436	87025	87616	88209	88804	89401
30	90000	90601	91204	91809	92416	93025	93636	94249	94864	95481
31	96100	96721	97344	97969	98596	99225	99856	100489	101124	101761
32	102400	103041	103684	104329	104976	105625	106276	106929	107584	108241
33	108900	109561	110224	110889	111556	112225	112896	113569	114244	114921
34	115600	116281	116964	117649	118336	119025	119716	120409	121104	121801
35	122500	123201	123904	124609	125316	126025	126736	127449	128164	128881
36	129600	130321	131044	131769	132496	133225	133956	134689	135424	136161
37	136900	137641	138384	139129	139876	140625	141376	142129	142884	143641
38	144400	145161	145924	146689	147456	148225	148996	149769	150544	151321
39	152100	152881	153664	154449	155236	156025	156816	157609	158404	159201
40	160000	160801	161604	162409	163216	164025	164836	165649	166464	167281
41	168100	168921	169744	170569	171396	172225	173056	173889	174724	175561
42	176400	177241	178084	178929	179776	180625	181476	182329	183184	184041
43	184900	185761	186624	187489	188356	189225	190096	190969	191844	192721
44	193600	194481	195364	196249	197136	198025	198916	199809	200704	201601
45	202500	203401	204304	205209	206116	207025	207936	208849	209764	210681
46	211600	212521	213444	214369	215296	216225	217156	218089	219024	219961
47	220900	221841	222784	223729	224676	225625	226576	227529	228484	229441
48	230400	231361	232324	233289	234256	235225	236196	237169	238144	239121
49	240100	241081	242064	243049	244036	245025	246016	247009	248004	249001

Exact squares of 4-figure numbers can be quickly calculated from the identity

$$(a \pm b)^2 = a^2 \pm 2ab + b^2$$

Squares

	0	1	2	3	4	5	6	7	8	9
50	250000	251001	252004	253009	254016	255025	256036	257049	258064	259081
51	260100	261121	262144	263169	264196	265225	266256	267289	268324	269361
52	270400	271441	272484	273529	274576	275625	276676	277729	278784	279841
53	280900	281961	283024	284089	285156	286225	287296	288369	289444	290521
54	291600	292681	293764	294849	295936	297025	298116	299209	300304	301401
55	302500	303601	304704	305809	306916	308025	309136	310249	311364	312481
56	313600	314721	315844	316969	318096	319225	320356	321489	322624	323761
57	324900	326041	327184	328329	329476	330625	331776	332929	334084	335241
58	336400	337561	338724	339889	341056	342225	343396	344569	345744	346921
59	348100	349281	350464	351649	352836	354025	355216	356409	357604	358801
60	360000	361201	362404	363609	364816	366025	367236	368449	369664	370881
61	372100	373321	374544	375769	376996	378225	379456	380689	381924	383161
62	384400	385641	386884	388129	389376	390625	391876	393129	394384	395641
63	396900	398161	399424	400689	401956	403225	404496	405769	407044	408321
64	409600	410881	412164	413449	414736	416025	417316	418609	419904	421201
65	422500	423801	425104	426409	427716	429025	430336	431649	432964	434281
66	435600	436921	438244	439569	440896	442225	443556	444889	446224	447561
67	448900	450241	451584	452929	454276	455625	456976	458329	459684	461041
68	462400	463761	465124	466489	467856	469225	470596	471969	473344	474721
69	476100	477481	478864	480249	481636	483025	484416	485809	487204	488601
70	490000	491401	492804	494209	495616	497025	498436	499849	501264	502681
71	504100	505521	506944	508369	509796	511225	512656	514089	515524	516961
72	518400	519841	521284	522729	524176	525625	527076	528529	529984	531441
73	532900	534361	535824	537289	538756	540225	541696	543169	544644	546121
74	547600	549081	550564	552049	553536	555025	556516	558009	559504	561001
75	562500	564001	565504	567009	568516	570025	571536	573049	574564	576081
76	577600	579121	580644	582169	583696	585225	586756	588289	589824	591361
77	592900	594441	595984	597529	599076	600625	602176	603729	605284	606841
78	608400	609961	611524	613089	614656	616225	617796	619369	620944	622521
79	624100	625681	627264	628849	630436	632025	633616	635209	636804	638401
80	640000	641601	643204	644809	646416	648025	649636	651249	652864	654481
81	656100	657721	659344	660969	662596	664225	665856	667489	669124	670761
82	672400	674041	675684	677329	678976	680625	682276	683929	685584	687241
83	688900	690561	692224	693889	695556	697225	698896	700569	702244	703921
84	705600	707281	708964	710649	712336	714025	715716	717409	719104	720801
85	722500	724201	725904	727609	729316	731025	732736	734449	736164	737881
86	739600	741321	743044	744769	746496	748225	749956	751689	753424	755161
87	756900	758641	760384	762129	763876	765625	767376	769129	770884	772641
88	774400	776161	777924	779689	781456	783225	784996	786769	788544	790321
89	792100	793881	795664	797449	799236	801025	802816	804609	806404	808201
90	810000	811801	813604	815409	817216	819025	820836	822649	824464	826281
91	828100	829941	831744	833569	835396	837225	839056	840889	842724	844561
92	846400	848241	850084	851929	853776	855625	857476	859329	861184	863041
93	864900	866761	868624	870489	872356	874225	876096	877969	879844	881721
94	883600	885481	887364	889249	891136	893025	894916	896809	898704	900601
95	902500	904401	906304	908209	910116	912025	913936	915849	917764	919681
96	921600	923521	925444	927369	929296	931225	933156	935089	937024	938961
97	940900	942841	944784	946729	948676	950625	952576	954529	956484	958441
98	960400	962361	964324	966289	968256	970225	972196	974169	976144	978121
99	980100	982081	984064	986049	988036	990025	992016	994009	996004	998001

Exact squares of 4-figure numbers can be quickly calculated from the identity

$$(a \pm b)^2 = a^2 \pm 2ab + b^2$$

Square Roots (From 1 to 10)

	0	1	2	3	4	5	6	7	8	9	Mean Differences								
											1	2	3	4	5	6	7	8	9
1.0	1.000	1.005	1.010	1.015	1.020	1.025	1.030	1.034	1.039	1.044	0	1	1	2	2	3	3	4	4
1.1	1.049	1.054	1.058	1.063	1.068	1.072	1.077	1.082	1.086	1.091	0	1	1	2	2	3	3	4	4
1.2	1.095	1.100	1.105	1.109	1.114	1.118	1.123	1.127	1.131	1.136	0	1	1	2	2	3	3	4	4
1.3	1.140	1.145	1.149	1.153	1.158	1.162	1.166	1.171	1.175	1.179	0	1	1	2	2	3	3	3	4
1.4	1.183	1.187	1.192	1.196	1.200	1.204	1.208	1.212	1.217	1.221	0	1	1	2	2	2	3	3	4
1.5	1.225	1.229	1.233	1.237	1.241	1.245	1.249	1.253	1.257	1.261	0	1	1	2	2	2	3	3	4
1.6	1.265	1.269	1.273	1.277	1.281	1.285	1.288	1.292	1.296	1.300	0	1	1	2	2	2	3	3	3
1.7	1.304	1.308	1.312	1.315	1.319	1.323	1.327	1.330	1.334	1.338	0	1	1	2	2	2	3	3	3
1.8	1.342	1.345	1.349	1.353	1.357	1.360	1.364	1.368	1.371	1.375	0	1	1	1	2	2	3	3	3
1.9	1.378	1.382	1.386	1.389	1.393	1.396	1.400	1.404	1.407	1.411	0	1	1	1	2	2	3	3	3
2.0	1.414	1.418	1.421	1.425	1.428	1.432	1.435	1.439	1.442	1.446	0	1	1	1	2	2	2	3	3
2.1	1.449	1.453	1.456	1.459	1.463	1.466	1.470	1.473	1.477	1.480	0	1	1	1	2	2	2	3	3
2.2	1.483	1.487	1.490	1.493	1.497	1.500	1.503	1.507	1.510	1.513	0	1	1	1	2	2	2	3	3
2.3	1.517	1.520	1.523	1.526	1.530	1.533	1.536	1.539	1.543	1.546	0	1	1	1	2	2	2	3	3
2.4	1.549	1.552	1.556	1.559	1.562	1.565	1.568	1.572	1.575	1.578	0	1	1	1	2	2	2	3	3
2.5	1.581	1.584	1.587	1.591	1.594	1.597	1.600	1.603	1.606	1.609	0	1	1	1	2	2	2	3	3
2.6	1.612	1.616	1.619	1.622	1.625	1.628	1.631	1.634	1.637	1.640	0	1	1	1	2	2	2	2	3
2.7	1.643	1.646	1.649	1.652	1.655	1.658	1.661	1.664	1.667	1.670	0	1	1	1	2	2	2	2	3
2.8	1.673	1.676	1.679	1.682	1.685	1.688	1.691	1.694	1.697	1.700	0	1	1	1	1	2	2	2	3
2.9	1.703	1.706	1.709	1.712	1.715	1.718	1.720	1.723	1.726	1.729	0	1	1	1	1	2	2	2	3
3.0	1.732	1.735	1.738	1.741	1.744	1.746	1.749	1.752	1.755	1.758	0	1	1	1	1	2	2	2	3
3.1	1.761	1.764	1.766	1.769	1.772	1.775	1.778	1.780	1.783	1.786	0	1	1	1	1	2	2	2	3
3.2	1.789	1.792	1.794	1.797	1.800	1.803	1.806	1.808	1.811	1.814	0	1	1	1	1	2	2	2	2
3.3	1.817	1.819	1.822	1.825	1.828	1.830	1.833	1.836	1.839	1.841	0	1	1	1	1	2	2	2	2
3.4	1.844	1.847	1.849	1.852	1.855	1.857	1.860	1.863	1.865	1.868	0	1	1	1	1	2	2	2	2
3.5	1.871	1.873	1.876	1.879	1.882	1.884	1.887	1.889	1.892	1.895	0	1	1	1	1	2	2	2	2
3.6	1.897	1.900	1.903	1.905	1.908	1.911	1.913	1.916	1.918	1.921	0	1	1	1	1	2	2	2	2
3.7	1.924	1.926	1.929	1.931	1.934	1.937	1.939	1.942	1.944	1.947	0	1	1	1	1	2	2	2	2
3.8	1.949	1.952	1.955	1.957	1.960	1.962	1.965	1.967	1.970	1.972	0	1	1	1	1	2	2	2	2
3.9	1.975	1.977	1.980	1.982	1.985	1.988	1.990	1.993	1.995	1.998	0	1	1	1	1	2	2	2	2
4.0	2.000	2.003	2.005	2.007	2.010	2.013	2.015	2.017	2.020	2.022	0	0	1	1	1	1	2	2	2
4.1	2.025	2.027	2.030	2.032	2.035	2.037	2.040	2.042	2.045	2.047	0	0	1	1	1	1	2	2	2
4.2	2.049	2.052	2.054	2.057	2.059	2.062	2.064	2.066	2.069	2.071	0	0	1	1	1	1	2	2	2
4.3	2.074	2.076	2.078	2.081	2.083	2.086	2.088	2.091	2.093	2.095	0	0	1	1	1	1	2	2	2
4.4	2.098	2.100	2.102	2.105	2.107	2.110	2.112	2.114	2.117	2.119	0	0	1	1	1	1	2	2	2
4.5	2.121	2.124	2.126	2.128	2.131	2.133	2.135	2.138	2.140	2.142	0	0	1	1	1	1	2	2	2
4.6	2.145	2.147	2.149	2.152	2.154	2.156	2.159	2.161	2.163	2.166	0	0	1	1	1	1	2	2	2
4.7	2.168	2.170	2.173	2.175	2.177	2.179	2.182	2.184	2.186	2.189	0	0	1	1	1	1	2	2	2
4.8	2.191	2.193	2.195	2.198	2.200	2.202	2.205	2.207	2.209	2.211	0	0	1	1	1	1	2	2	2
4.9	2.214	2.216	2.218	2.220	2.223	2.225	2.227	2.229	2.232	2.234	0	0	1	1	1	1	2	2	2
5.0	2.236	2.238	2.241	2.243	2.245	2.247	2.249	2.252	2.254	2.256	0	0	1	1	1	1	2	2	2
5.1	2.258	2.261	2.263	2.265	2.267	2.269	2.272	2.274	2.276	2.278	0	0	1	1	1	1	2	2	2
5.2	2.280	2.283	2.285	2.287	2.289	2.291	2.293	2.296	2.298	2.300	0	0	1	1	1	1	2	2	2
5.3	2.302	2.304	2.307	2.309	2.311	2.313	2.315	2.317	2.320	2.322	0	0	1	1	1	1	2	2	2
5.4	2.324	2.326	2.328	2.330	2.332	2.335	2.337	2.339	2.341	2.343	0	0	1	1	1	1	1	2	2

$\sqrt{1.856} \doteqdot 1.360 + 0.002 \doteqdot 1.362$

$\sqrt{185.6} \doteqdot \sqrt{1.856 \times 10^2} \doteqdot 1.362 \times 10 \doteqdot 13.62$

$\sqrt{0.01856} \doteqdot \sqrt{1.856 \times 10^{-2}} \doteqdot 1.362 \times 10^{-1} \doteqdot 0.1362$

Note that the power of 10 extracted under the root sign must always be even.

Square Roots (From 1 to 10)

	0	1	2	3	4	5	6	7	8	9	Mean Differences 1	2	3	4	5	6	7	8	9
5.5	2.345	2.347	2.350	2.352	2.354	2.356	2.358	2.360	2.362	2.364	0	0	1	1	1	1	1	2	2
5.6	2.366	2.369	2.371	2.373	2.375	2.377	2.379	2.381	2.383	2.385	0	0	1	1	1	1	1	2	2
5.7	2.387	2.390	2.392	2.394	2.396	2.398	2.400	2.402	2.404	2.406	0	0	1	1	1	1	1	2	2
5.8	2.408	2.410	2.412	2.415	2.417	2.419	2.421	2.423	2.425	2.427	0	0	1	1	1	1	1	2	2
5.9	2.429	2.431	2.433	2.435	2.437	2.439	2.441	2.443	2.445	2.447	0	0	1	1	1	1	1	2	2
6.0	2.450	2.452	2.454	2.456	2.458	2.460	2.462	2.464	2.466	2.468	0	0	1	1	1	1	1	2	2
6.1	2.470	2.472	2.474	2.476	2.478	2.480	2.482	2.484	2.486	2.488	0	0	1	1	1	1	1	2	2
6.2	2.490	2.492	2.494	2.496	2.498	2.500	2.502	2.504	2.506	2.508	0	0	1	1	1	1	1	2	2
6.3	2.510	2.512	2.514	2.516	2.518	2.520	2.522	2.524	2.526	2.528	0	0	1	1	1	1	1	2	2
6.4	2.530	2.532	2.534	2.536	2.538	2.540	2.542	2.544	2.546	2.548	0	0	1	1	1	1	1	2	2
6.5	2.550	2.551	2.553	2.555	2.557	2.559	2.561	2.563	2.565	2.567	0	0	1	1	1	1	1	2	2
6.6	2.569	2.571	2.573	2.575	2.577	2.579	2.581	2.583	2.585	2.587	0	0	1	1	1	1	1	2	2
6.7	2.588	2.590	2.592	2.594	2.596	2.598	2.600	2.602	2.604	2.606	0	0	1	1	1	1	1	2	2
6.8	2.608	2.610	2.612	2.613	2.615	2.617	2.619	2.621	2.623	2.625	0	0	1	1	1	1	1	2	2
6.9	2.627	2.629	2.631	2.632	2.634	2.636	2.638	2.640	2.642	2.644	0	0	1	1	1	1	1	2	2
7.0	2.646	2.648	2.650	2.651	2.653	2.655	2.657	2.659	2.661	2.663	0	0	1	1	1	1	1	2	2
7.1	2.665	2.667	2.668	2.670	2.672	2.674	2.676	2.678	2.680	2.681	0	0	1	1	1	1	1	1	2
7.2	2.683	2.685	2.687	2.689	2.691	2.693	2.694	2.696	2.698	2.700	0	0	1	1	1	1	1	1	2
7.3	2.702	2.704	2.706	2.707	2.709	2.711	2.713	2.715	2.717	2.718	0	0	1	1	1	1	1	1	2
7.4	2.720	2.722	2.724	2.726	2.728	2.729	2.731	2.733	2.735	2.737	0	0	1	1	1	1	1	1	2
7.5	2.739	2.740	2.742	2.744	2.746	2.748	2.750	2.751	2.753	2.755	0	0	1	1	1	1	1	1	2
7.6	2.757	2.759	2.760	2.762	2.764	2.766	2.768	2.769	2.771	2.773	0	0	1	1	1	1	1	1	2
7.7	2.775	2.777	2.778	2.780	2.782	2.784	2.786	2.787	2.789	2.791	0	0	1	1	1	1	1	1	2
7.8	2.793	2.795	2.796	2.798	2.800	2.802	2.804	2.805	2.807	2.809	0	0	1	1	1	1	1	1	2
7.9	2.811	2.812	2.814	2.816	2.818	2.820	2.821	2.823	2.825	2.827	0	0	1	1	1	1	1	1	2
8.0	2.828	2.830	2.832	2.834	2.835	2.837	2.839	2.841	2.843	2.844	0	0	1	1	1	1	1	1	2
8.1	2.846	2.848	2.850	2.851	2.853	2.855	2.857	2.858	2.860	2.862	0	0	1	1	1	1	1	1	2
8.2	2.864	2.865	2.867	2.869	2.871	2.872	2.874	2.876	2.877	2.879	0	0	1	1	1	1	1	1	2
8.3	2.881	2.883	2.884	2.886	2.888	2.890	2.891	2.893	2.895	2.897	0	0	1	1	1	1	1	1	2
8.4	2.898	2.900	2.902	2.903	2.905	2.907	2.909	2.910	2.912	2.914	0	0	1	1	1	1	1	1	2
8.5	2.915	2.917	2.919	2.921	2.922	2.924	2.926	2.927	2.929	2.931	0	0	1	1	1	1	1	1	2
8.6	2.933	2.934	2.936	2.938	2.939	2.941	2.943	2.944	2.946	2.948	0	0	1	1	1	1	1	1	2
8.7	2.950	2.951	2.953	2.955	2.956	2.958	2.960	2.961	2.963	2.965	0	0	1	1	1	1	1	1	2
8.8	2.966	2.968	2.970	2.972	2.973	2.975	2.977	2.978	2.980	2.982	0	0	1	1	1	1	1	1	2
8.9	2.983	2.985	2.987	2.988	2.990	2.992	2.993	2.995	2.997	2.998	0	0	1	1	1	1	1	1	2
9.0	3.000	3.002	3.003	3.005	3.007	3.008	3.010	3.012	3.013	3.015	0	0	0	1	1	1	1	1	1
9.1	3.017	3.018	3.020	3.022	3.023	3.025	3.027	3.028	3.030	3.032	0	0	0	1	1	1	1	1	1
9.2	3.033	3.035	3.036	3.038	3.040	3.041	3.043	3.045	3.046	3.048	0	0	0	1	1	1	1	1	1
9.3	3.050	3.051	3.053	3.055	3.056	3.058	3.059	3.061	3.063	3.064	0	0	0	1	1	1	1	1	1
9.4	3.066	3.068	3.069	3.071	3.072	3.074	3.076	3.077	3.079	3.081	0	0	0	1	1	1	1	1	1
9.5	3.082	3.084	3.085	3.087	3.089	3.090	3.092	3.094	3.095	3.097	0	0	0	1	1	1	1	1	1
9.6	3.098	3.100	3.102	3.103	3.105	3.106	3.108	3.110	3.111	3.113	0	0	0	1	1	1	1	1	1
9.7	3.115	3.116	3.118	3.119	3.121	3.123	3.124	3.126	3.127	3.129	0	0	0	1	1	1	1	1	1
9.8	3.131	3.132	3.134	3.135	3.137	3.139	3.140	3.142	3.143	3.145	0	0	0	1	1	1	1	1	1
9.9	3.146	3.148	3.150	3.151	3.153	3.154	3.156	3.158	3.159	3.161	0	0	0	1	1	1	1	1	1

Square Roots (From 10 to 100)

	0	1	2	3	4	5	6	7	8	9	Mean Differences								
											1	2	3	4	5	6	7	8	9
10	3.162	3.178	3.194	3.209	3.225	3.240	3.256	3.271	3.286	3.302	2	3	5	6	8	9	11	12	14
11	3.317	3.332	3.347	3.362	3.376	3.391	3.406	3.421	3.435	3.450	1	3	4	6	7	9	10	12	13
12	3.464	3.479	3.493	3.507	3.521	3.536	3.550	3.564	3.578	3.592	1	3	4	6	7	8	10	11	13
13	3.606	3.619	3.633	3.647	3.661	3.674	3.688	3.701	3.715	3.728	1	3	4	5	7	8	10	11	12
14	3.742	3.755	3.768	3.782	3.795	3.808	3.821	3.834	3.847	3.860	1	3	4	5	7	8	9	11	12
15	3.873	3.886	3.899	3.912	3.924	3.937	3.950	3.962	3.975	3.988	1	3	4	5	6	8	9	10	11
16	4.000	4.012	4.025	4.037	4.050	4.062	4.074	4.087	4.099	4.111	1	2	4	5	6	7	9	10	11
17	4.123	4.135	4.147	4.159	4.171	4.183	4.195	4.207	4.219	4.231	1	2	4	5	6	7	8	10	11
18	4.243	4.254	4.266	4.278	4.290	4.301	4.313	4.324	4.336	4.347	1	2	3	5	6	7	8	9	10
19	4.359	4.370	4.382	4.393	4.405	4.416	4.427	4.438	4.450	4.461	1	2	3	5	6	7	8	9	10
20	4.472	4.483	4.494	4.506	4.517	4.528	4.539	4.550	4.561	4.572	1	2	3	4	6	7	8	9	10
21	4.583	4.594	4.604	4.615	4.626	4.637	4.648	4.658	4.669	4.680	1	2	3	4	5	6	8	9	10
22	4.690	4.701	4.712	4.722	4.733	4.743	4.754	4.765	4.775	4.785	1	2	3	4	5	6	7	8	9
23	4.796	4.806	4.817	4.827	4.837	4.848	4.858	4.868	4.879	4.889	1	2	3	4	5	6	7	8	9
24	4.899	4.909	4.919	4.930	4.940	4.950	4.960	4.970	4.980	4.990	1	2	3	4	5	6	7	8	9
25	5.000	5.010	5.020	5.030	5.040	5.050	5.060	5.070	5.079	5.089	1	2	3	4	5	6	7	8	9
26	5.099	5.109	5.119	5.128	5.138	5.148	5.158	5.167	5.177	5.187	1	2	3	4	5	6	7	8	9
27	5.196	5.206	5.215	5.225	5.235	5.244	5.254	5.263	5.273	5.282	1	2	3	4	5	6	7	8	9
28	5.292	5.301	5.310	5.320	5.329	5.339	5.348	5.357	5.367	5.376	1	2	3	4	5	6	7	7	8
29	5.385	5.394	5.404	5.413	5.422	5.431	5.441	5.450	5.459	5.468	1	2	3	4	5	5	6	7	8
30	5.477	5.486	5.495	5.505	5.514	5.523	5.532	5.541	5.550	5.559	1	2	3	4	4	5	6	7	8
31	5.568	5.577	5.586	5.595	5.604	5.612	5.621	5.630	5.639	5.648	1	2	3	3	4	5	6	7	8
32	5.657	5.666	5.675	5.683	5.692	5.701	5.710	5.718	5.727	5.736	1	2	3	3	4	5	6	7	8
33	5.745	5.753	5.762	5.771	5.779	5.788	5.797	5.805	5.814	5.822	1	2	3	3	4	5	6	7	8
34	5.831	5.840	5.848	5.857	5.865	5.874	5.882	5.891	5.899	5.908	1	2	3	3	4	5	6	7	8
35	5.916	5.925	5.933	5.941	5.950	5.958	5.967	5.975	5.983	5.992	1	2	2	3	4	5	6	7	8
36	6.000	6.008	6.017	6.025	6.033	6.042	6.050	6.058	6.066	6.075	1	2	2	3	4	5	6	7	7
37	6.083	6.091	6.099	6.107	6.116	6.124	6.132	6.140	6.148	6.156	1	2	2	3	4	5	6	7	7
38	6.164	6.173	6.181	6.189	6.197	6.205	6.213	6.221	6.229	6.237	1	2	2	3	4	5	6	6	7
39	6.245	6.253	6.261	6.269	6.277	6.285	6.293	6.301	6.309	6.317	1	2	2	3	4	5	6	6	7
40	6.325	6.332	6.340	6.348	6.356	6.364	6.372	6.380	6.387	6.395	1	2	2	3	4	5	6	6	7
41	6.403	6.411	6.419	6.427	6.434	6.442	6.450	6.458	6.465	6.473	1	2	2	3	4	5	5	6	7
42	6.481	6.488	6.496	6.504	6.512	6.519	6.527	6.535	6.542	6.550	1	2	2	3	4	5	5	6	7
43	6.557	6.565	6.573	6.580	6.588	6.595	6.603	6.611	6.618	6.626	1	2	2	3	4	5	5	6	7
44	6.633	6.641	6.648	6.656	6.663	6.671	6.678	6.686	6.693	6.701	1	2	2	3	4	5	5	6	7
45	6.708	6.716	6.723	6.731	6.738	6.745	6.753	6.760	6.768	6.775	1	1	2	3	4	4	5	6	7
46	6.782	6.790	6.797	6.804	6.812	6.819	6.826	6.834	6.841	6.848	1	1	2	3	4	4	5	6	7
47	6.856	6.863	6.870	6.878	6.885	6.892	6.899	6.907	6.914	6.921	1	1	2	3	4	4	5	6	7
48	6.928	6.935	6.943	6.950	6.957	6.964	6.971	6.979	6.986	6.993	1	1	2	3	4	4	5	6	6
49	7.000	7.007	7.014	7.021	7.029	7.036	7.043	7.050	7.057	7.064	1	1	2	3	4	4	5	6	6
50	7.071	7.078	7.085	7.092	7.099	7.106	7.113	7.120	7.127	7.134	1	1	2	3	4	4	5	6	6
51	7.141	7.148	7.155	7.162	7.169	7.176	7.183	7.190	7.197	7.204	1	1	2	3	4	4	5	6	6
52	7.211	7.218	7.225	7.232	7.239	7.246	7.253	7.259	7.266	7.273	1	1	2	3	3	4	5	6	6
53	7.280	7.287	7.294	7.301	7.308	7.314	7.321	7.328	7.335	7.342	1	1	2	3	3	4	5	5	6
54	7.349	7.355	7.362	7.369	7.376	7.382	7.389	7.396	7.403	7.410	1	1	2	3	3	4	5	5	6

$\sqrt{18.56} \doteqdot 4.301 + 0.007 \doteqdot 4.308$

$\sqrt{1856} \doteqdot \sqrt{18.56 \times 10^2} \doteqdot 4.308 \times 10^1 \doteqdot 43.08$

$\sqrt{0.1856} \doteqdot \sqrt{18.56 \times 10^{-2}} \doteqdot 4.308 \times 10^{-1} \doteqdot 0.4308$

Note that the power of 10 extracted under the root sign must always be even.

Square Roots (From 10 to 100)

	0	1	2	3	4	5	6	7	8	9	Mean Differences								
											1	2	3	4	5	6	7	8	9
55	7.416	7.423	7.430	7.436	7.443	7.450	7.457	7.463	7.470	7.477	1	1	2	3	3	4	5	5	6
56	7.483	7.490	7.497	7.503	7.510	7.517	7.523	7.530	7.537	7.543	1	1	2	3	3	4	5	5	6
57	7.550	7.556	7.563	7.570	7.576	7.583	7.589	7.596	7.603	7.609	1	1	2	3	3	4	5	5	6
58	7.616	7.622	7.629	7.635	7.642	7.649	7.655	7.662	7.668	7.675	1	1	2	3	3	4	5	5	6
59	7.681	7.688	7.694	7.701	7.707	7.714	7.720	7.727	7.733	7.740	1	1	2	3	3	4	4	5	6
60	7.746	7.752	7.759	7.765	7.772	7.778	7.785	7.791	7.797	7.804	1	1	2	3	3	4	4	5	6
61	7.810	7.817	7.823	7.829	7.836	7.842	7.849	7.855	7.861	7.868	1	1	2	3	3	4	4	5	6
62	7.874	7.880	7.887	7.893	7.899	7.906	7.912	7.918	7.925	7.931	1	1	2	3	3	4	4	5	6
63	7.937	7.944	7.950	7.956	7.962	7.969	7.975	7.981	7.987	7.994	1	1	2	3	3	4	4	5	6
64	8.000	8.006	8.012	8.019	8.025	8.031	8.037	8.044	8.050	8.056	1	1	2	2	3	4	4	5	6
65	8.062	8.068	8.075	8.081	8.087	8.093	8.099	8.106	8.112	8.118	1	1	2	2	3	4	4	5	6
66	8.124	8.130	8.136	8.142	8.149	8.155	8.161	8.167	8.173	8.179	1	1	2	2	3	4	4	5	5
67	8.185	8.191	8.198	8.204	8.210	8.216	8.222	8.228	8.234	8.240	1	1	2	2	3	4	4	5	5
68	8.246	8.252	8.258	8.264	8.270	8.276	8.283	8.289	8.295	8.301	1	1	2	2	3	4	4	5	5
69	8.307	8.313	8.319	8.325	8.331	8.337	8.343	8.349	8.355	8.361	1	1	2	2	3	4	4	5	5
70	8.367	8.373	8.379	8.385	8.390	8.396	8.402	8.408	8.414	8.420	1	1	2	2	3	4	4	5	5
71	8.426	8.432	8.438	8.444	8.450	8.456	8.462	8.468	8.473	8.479	1	1	2	2	3	4	4	5	5
72	8.485	8.491	8.497	8.503	8.509	8.515	8.521	8.526	8.532	8.538	1	1	2	2	3	3	4	5	5
73	8.544	8.550	8.556	8.562	8.567	8.573	8.579	8.585	8.591	8.597	1	1	2	2	3	3	4	5	5
74	8.602	8.608	8.614	8.620	8.626	8.631	8.637	8.643	8.649	8.654	1	1	2	2	3	3	4	5	5
75	8.660	8.666	8.672	8.678	8.683	8.689	8.695	8.701	8.706	8.712	1	1	2	2	3	3	4	5	5
76	8.718	8.724	8.729	8.735	8.741	8.746	8.752	8.758	8.764	8.769	1	1	2	2	3	3	4	5	5
77	8.775	8.781	8.786	8.792	8.798	8.803	8.809	8.815	8.820	8.826	1	1	2	2	3	3	4	4	5
78	8.832	8.837	8.843	8.849	8.854	8.860	8.866	8.871	8.877	8.883	1	1	2	2	3	3	4	4	5
79	8.888	8.894	8.899	8.905	8.911	8.916	8.922	8.927	8.933	8.939	1	1	2	2	3	3	4	4	5
80	8.944	8.950	8.955	8.961	8.967	8.972	8.978	8.983	8.989	8.994	1	1	2	2	3	3	4	4	5
81	9.000	9.006	9.011	9.017	9.022	9.028	9.033	9.039	9.044	9.050	1	1	2	2	3	3	4	4	5
82	9.055	9.061	9.066	9.072	9.077	9.083	9.088	9.094	9.099	9.105	1	1	2	2	3	3	4	4	5
83	9.110	9.116	9.121	9.127	9.132	9.138	9.143	9.149	9.154	9.160	1	1	2	2	3	3	4	4	5
84	9.165	9.171	9.176	9.182	9.187	9.192	9.198	9.203	9.209	9.214	1	1	2	2	3	3	4	4	5
85	9.220	9.225	9.230	9.236	9.241	9.247	9.252	9.257	9.263	9.268	1	1	2	2	3	3	4	4	5
86	9.274	9.279	9.284	9.290	9.295	9.301	9.306	9.311	9.317	9.322	1	1	2	2	3	3	4	4	5
87	9.327	9.333	9.338	9.343	9.349	9.354	9.359	9.365	9.370	9.375	1	1	2	2	3	3	4	4	5
88	9.381	9.386	9.391	9.397	9.402	9.407	9.413	9.418	9.423	9.429	1	1	2	2	3	3	4	4	5
89	9.434	9.439	9.445	9.450	9.455	9.460	9.466	9.471	9.476	9.482	1	1	2	2	3	3	4	4	5
90	9.487	9.492	9.497	9.503	9.508	9.513	9.518	9.524	9.529	9.534	1	1	2	2	3	3	4	4	5
91	9.539	9.545	9.550	9.555	9.560	9.566	9.571	9.576	9.581	9.586	1	1	2	2	3	3	4	4	5
92	9.592	9.597	9.602	9.607	9.613	9.618	9.623	9.628	9.633	9.638	1	1	2	2	3	3	4	4	5
93	9.644	9.649	9.654	9.659	9.664	9.670	9.675	9.680	9.685	9.690	1	1	2	2	3	3	4	4	5
94	9.695	9.701	9.706	9.711	9.716	9.721	9.726	9.731	9.737	9.742	1	1	2	2	3	3	4	4	5
95	9.747	9.752	9.757	9.762	9.767	9.772	9.778	9.783	9.788	9.793	1	1	2	2	3	3	4	4	5
96	9.798	9.803	9.808	9.813	9.818	9.823	9.829	9.834	9.839	9.844	1	1	2	2	3	3	4	4	5
97	9.849	9.854	9.859	9.864	9.869	9.874	9.879	9.884	9.889	9.894	1	1	1	2	3	3	4	4	5
98	9.900	9.905	9.910	9.915	9.920	9.925	9.930	9.935	9.940	9.945	0	1	1	2	2	3	3	4	4
99	9.950	9.955	9.960	9.965	9.970	9.975	9.980	9.985	9.990	9.995	0	1	1	2	2	3	3	4	4

Powers and Factorials

x	x^2	x^3	$10/x$	$\sqrt{x}$	$1/\sqrt{x}$	$\sqrt[3]{x}$	Δ	$\sqrt[3]{10x}$	Δ	$\sqrt[3]{100x}$	Δ	$x!$	c
							+ Use $\frac{1}{10}\sqrt[3]{100y}$, y = 10x		+ Use $\sqrt[3]{y}$, y = 10x		+ Use $\sqrt[3]{y}$, y = 10x		*
1	1	1	10	1.000	1.0000	1.000		2.154		4.642		1	
2	4	8	5	1.414	0.7071	1.260		2.714		5.848		2	
3	9	27	3.333	1.732	.5774	1.442		3.107		5.694		6	
4	16	64	2.5	2.000	.5000	1.587		3.420		7.368		24	
5	25	125	2	2.236	.4472	1.710		3.684		7.937		120	
6	36	216	1.667	2.449	.4082	1.817		3.915		8.434		720	
7	49	343	1.429	2.646	.3780	1.913		4.121		8.879		5.040	3
8	64	512	1.25	2.828	.3536	2.000		4.309		9.283		4.032	4
9	81	729	1.111	3.000	.3333	2.080		4.481		9.655		3.629	5
10	100	1000	1	3.162	.3162	2.154	70	4.642	149 †	10.00	32	3.629	6
11	121	1331	.9091	3.317	.3015	2.224	65	4.791	134 †	10.32	31	3.992	7
12	144	1728	.8333	3.464	.2887	2.289	62	4.932	134 †	10.63	28	4.790	8
13	169	2197	.7692	3.606	.2774	2.351	59	5.066	126	10.91	28	6.227	9
14	196	2744	.7143	3.742	.2673	2.410	56	5.192	121	11.19	26	8.718	10
15	225	3375	.6667	3.873	.2582	2.466	54	5.313	116	11.45	25	1.308	12
16	256	4096	.6250	4.000	.2500	2.520	51	5.429	111	11.70	23	2.092	13
17	289	4913	.5882	4.123	.2425	2.571	50	5.540	106	11.93	23	3.557	14
18	324	5832	.5556	4.243	.2357	2.621	47	5.646	103	12.16	23	6.402	15
19	361	6859	.5263	4.359	.2294	2.668	46	5.749	99	12.39	21	1.216	17
20	400	8000	.5000	4.472	.2236	2.714	45	5.848	96	12.60	21	2.433	18
21	441	9261	.4762	4.583	.2182	2.759	43	5.944	93	12.81	20	5.109	19
22	484	10648	.4545	4.690	.2132	2.802	42	6.037	90	13.01	19	1.124	21
23	529	12167	.4348	4.796	.2085	2.844	40	6.127	87	13.20	19	2.585	22
24	576	13824	.4167	4.899	.2041	2.884	40	6.214	86	13.39	18	6.204	23
25	625	15625	.4000	5.000	.2000	2.924	38	6.300	83	13.57	18	1.551	25
26	676	17576	.3846	5.099	.1961	2.962	38	6.383	80	13.75	17	4.033	26
27	729	19683	.3704	5.196	.1925	3.000	37	6.463	79	13.92	17	1.089	28
28	784	21952	.3571	5.292	.1890	3.037	35	6.542	77	14.09	17	3.049	29
29	841	24389	.3448	5.385	.1857	3.072	35	6.619	75	14.26	16	8.842	30
30	900	27000	.3333	5.477	.1826	3.107	34	6.694	74	14.42	16	2.653	32
31	961	29791	.3226	5.568	.1796	3.141	34	6.768	72	14.58	16	8.223	33
32	1024	32768	.3125	5.657	.1768	3.175	33	6.840	70	14.74	15	2.631	35
33	1089	35937	.3030	5.745	.1741	3.208	32	6.910	70	14.89	15	8.683	36
34	1156	39304	.2941	5.831	.1751	3.240	31	6.980	67	15.04	14	2.952	38
35	1225	42875	.2857	5.916	.1690	3.271	31	7.047	67	15.18	15	1.033	40
36	1296	46656	.2778	6.000	.1667	3.302	30	7.114	65	15.33	14	3.720	41
37	1369	50653	.2703	6.083	.1644	3.332	30	7.179	64	15.47	13	1.376	43
38	1444	54872	.2632	6.164	.1622	3.362	29	7.243	63	15.60	14	5.230	44
39	1521	59319	.2564	6.245	.1601	3.391	29	7.306	62	15.74	13	2.040	46
40	1600	64000	.2500	6.325	.1581	3.420	28	7.368	61	15.87	14	8.159	47
41	1681	68921	.2439	6.403	.1562	3.448	28	7.429	60	16.01	12	3.345	49
42	1764	74088	.2381	6.481	.1543	3.476	27	7.489	59	16.13	13	1.405	51
43	1849	79507	.2326	6.557	.1525	3.503	27	7.548	58	16.26	13	6.042	52
44	1936	85184	.2273	6.633	.1508	3.530	27	7.606	57	16.39	12	2.658	54
45	2025	91125	.2222	6.708	.1491	3.557	26	7.663	56	16.51	12	1.196	56
46	2116	97336	.2174	6.782	.1474	3.583	26	7.719	56	16.63	12	5.503	57
47	2209	103823	.2128	6.856	.1459	3.609	25	7.775	55	16.75	12	2.586	59
48	2304	110592	.2083	6.928	.1443	3.634	25	7.830	54	16.87	11	1.241	61
49	2401	117649	.2041	7.000	.1429	3.659	25	7.884	53	16.98	12	6.083	62

Powers and Factorials

x	x^2	x^3	$10/x$	$\sqrt{x}$	$1/\sqrt{x}$	$\sqrt[3]{x}$	Δ	$\sqrt[3]{10x}$	Δ	$\sqrt[3]{100x}$	Δ	$x!$	c
							+		+		+		*
50	2500	125000	.2000	7.071	.1414	3.684	24	7.937	53	17.10	11	3.041	64
51	2601	132651	.1961	7.141	.1400	3.708	25	7.990	51	17.21	11	1.551	66
52	2704	140608	.1923	7.211	.1387	3.733	23	8.041	52	17.32	12	8.066	67
53	2809	148877	.1887	7.280	.1374	3.756	24	8.093	50	17.44	10	4.275	69
54	2916	157464	.1852	7.348	.1361	3.780	23	8.143	50	17.54	11	2.308	71
55	3025	166375	.1818	7.416	.1348	3.803	23	8.193	50	17.65	11	1.270	73
56	3136	175616	.1786	7.483	.1336	3.826	23	8.243	48	17.76	10	7.110	74
57	3249	185193	.1754	7.550	.1325	3.849	22	8.291	49	17.86	11	4.053	76
58	3364	195112	.1724	7.616	.1313	3.871	22	8.340	47	17.97	10	2.351	78
59	3481	205379	.1695	7.681	.1302	3.893	22	8.387	47	18.07	10	1.387	80
60	3600	216000	.1667	7.746	.1291	3.915	21	8.434	47	18.17	10	8.321	81
61	3721	226981	.1639	7.810	.1280	3.936	22	8.481	46	18.27	10	5.076	83
62	3844	238328	.1613	7.874	.1270	3.958	21	8.527	46	18.37	10	3.147	85
63	3969	250047	.1587	7.937	.1260	3.979	21	8.573	45	18.47	10	1.983	87
64	4096	262144	.1562	8.000	.1250	4.000	21	8.618	44	18.57	9	1.269	89
65	4225	274625	.1538	8.062	.1240	4.021	20	8.662	45	18.66	10	8.248	90
66	4356	287496	.1515	8.124	.1231	4.041	21	8.707	43	18.76	9	5.443	92
67	4489	300763	.1493	8.185	.1222	4.062	20	8.750	44	18.85	10	3.647	94
68	4624	314432	.1471	8.246	.1213	4.082	20	8.794	43	18.95	9	2.480	96
69	4761	328509	.1449	8.307	.1204	4.102	19	8.837	42	19.04	9	1.711	98
70	4900	343000	.1429	8.367	.1195	4.121	20	8.879	42	19.13	9	1.198	100
71	5041	357911	.1408	8.426	.1187	4.141	19	8.921	42	19.22	9	8.505	101
72	5184	373248	.1389	8.485	.1179	4.160	19	8.963	41	19.31	9	6.123	103
73	5329	389017	.1370	8.544	.1170	4.179	19	9.004	41	19.40	9	4.470	105
74	5476	405224	.1351	8.602	.1162	4.198	19	9.045	41	19.49	8	3.308	107
75	5625	421875	.1333	8.660	.1155	4.217	19	9.086	40	19.57	9	2.481	109
76	5776	438976	.1316	8.718	.1147	4.236	18	9.126	40	19.66	9	1.885	111
77	5929	456533	.1299	8.775	.1140	4.254	19	9.166	39	19.75	8	1.452	113
78	6084	474552	.1282	8.832	.1132	4.273	18	9.205	39	19.83	9	1.132	115
79	6241	493039	.1266	8.888	.1125	4.291	18	9.244	39	19.92	8	8.946	116
80	6400	512000	.1250	8.944	.1118	4.309	18	9.283	39	20.00	8	7.157	118
81	6561	531441	.1235	9.000	.1111	4.327	17	9.322	38	20.08	9	5.797	120
82	6724	551368	.1220	9.055	.1104	4.344	18	9.360	38	20.17	8	4.754	122
83	6889	571787	.1205	9.110	.1098	4.362	18	9.398	37	20.25	8	3.946	124
84	7056	592704	.1190	9.165	.1091	4.380	17	9.435	38	20.33	8	3.314	126
85	7225	614125	.1176	9.220	.1085	4.397	17	9.473	37	20.41	8	2.817	128
86	7396	636056	.1163	9.274	.1078	4.414	17	9.510	36	20.49	8	2.423	130
87	7569	658503	.1149	9.327	.1072	4.431	17	9.546	37	20.57	8	2.108	132
88	7744	681472	.1136	9.381	.1066	4.448	17	9.583	36	20.65	7	1.855	134
89	7921	704969	.1124	9.434	.1060	4.465	16	9.619	36	20.72	8	1.651	136
90	8100	729000	.1111	9.487	.1054	4.481	17	9.655	36	20.80	8	1.486	138
91	8281	753571	.1099	9.539	.1048	4.498	16	9.691	35	20.88	7	1.352	140
92	8464	778688	.1087	9.592	.1043	4.514	17	9.726	35	20.95	8	1.244	142
93	8649	804357	.1075	9.644	.1037	4.531	16	9.761	35	21.03	7	1.157	144
94	8836	830584	.1064	9.695	.1031	4.547	16	9.796	34	21.10	8	1.087	146
95	9025	857375	.1053	9.747	.1026	4.563	16	9.830	35	21.18	7	1.033	148
96	9216	884736	.1042	9.798	.1021	4.579	16	9.865	34	21.25	8	9.917	149
97	9409	912673	.1031	9.849	.1015	4.595	15	9.899	34	21.33	7	9.619	151
98	9604	941192	.1020	9.899	.1010	4.610	16	9.933	34	21.40	7	9.427	153
99	9801	970299	.1010	9.950	.1005	4.626	16	9.967	33	21.47	7	9.333	155

SYMBOLS, DIMENSIONS AND UNITS FOR PHYSICAL QUANTITIES

Quantity	Symbol	Dimension	Units
1. Length	L	L	metre (m)
2. Mass	M	M	kilogram (kg)
3. Time	T	T	second (s)
4. Current	I	I	ampere (A)
5. Temperature	T	Θ	kelvin (K)
6. Area	A	L^2	m^2
7. Volume	V	L^3	m^3
8. Wavelength	λ	L	m
9. Displacement	s	L	m
10. Velocity	v	LT^{-1}	m/s
11. Acceleration	a	LT^{-2}	m/s^2
12. Momentum	P	MLT^{-1}	kg·m/s
13. Force	F	MLT^{-2}	newton (N), $kg{\cdot}m/s^2$
14. Work	W	ML^2T^{-2}	joule (J)
15. Energy	E	ML^2T^{-2}	J
16. Power	P	ML^2T^{-3}	watt (W), J/s
17. Density	ρ	ML^{-3}	kg/m^3
18. Period	T	T	s
19. Frequency	f, ν	T^{-1}	hertz (Hz)
20. Angular Displacement	θ	—	radian (rad)
21. Angular velocity	ω	T^{-1}	rad/s
22. Angular speed and Angular Frequency	ω	T^{-1}	rad/s
23. Angular Momentum	L	ML^2T^{-1}	$kg{\cdot}m^2/s$
24. Angular Acceleration	α	T^{-2}	rad/s^2
25. Torque	τ	ML^2T^{-2}	N·m
26. Rotational inertia	I	ML^2	$kg{\cdot}m^2$
27. Gravitational field strength	g	LT^{-2}	N/kg
28. Gravitational potential	V	L^2T^{-2}	J/kg
29. Pressure	p	$ML^{-1}T^{-2}$	N/m^2, pascal (Pa)
30. Stress	p	$ML^{-1}T^{-2}$	N/m^2
31. Surface tension	T	MT^{-2}	N/m
32. Heat	Q	ML^2T^{-2}	J
33. Internal energy	U or E	ML^2T^{-2}	J
34. Specific heat	C	$L^2T^{-2}\Theta^{-1}$	J/kg·K
35. Latent heat	L	L^2T^{-2}	J/kg
36. Thermal Conductivity	K	MLT^{-3}	$\frac{W}{m{\cdot}k}$
37. Entropy	S	ML^2T^{-2}	J/K
38. Charge	Q	IT	coulomb (C)
39. Voltage	V	$ML^2T^{-3}I^{-1}$	volt (V)
40. Resistance	R	$ML^2T^{-3}I^{-2}$	ohm (Ω)
41. Resistivity	ρ	$ML^3T^{-3}I^{-2}$	$\Omega{\cdot}m$
42. Electrical conductivity	σ	$M^{-1}L^{-3}T^3I^2$	siemens/metre
43. Electromotive force	e	$ML^2T^{-3}I^{-1}$	V
44. Electric field strength	E	$MLT^{-3}I^{-1}$	N/C, V/m
45. Electric potential	V	$ML^2T^{-3}I^{-1}$	V
46. Electric potential gradient	k	$MLT^{-3}I^{-1}$	V/m
47. Capacitance	C	$M^{-1}L^{-2}T^4I^2$	farad (F)
48. Current density	j	IL^{-2}	A/m^2
49. Electric dipole moment	P	LIT	C·m
50. Electric displacement	D	$L^{-2}IT$	C/m^2
51. Electric polarization	P	$L^{-2}IT$	C/m^2
52. Electric flux	Φ_E	$ML^3T^{-3}I^{-1}$	$N{\cdot}m^2/C$
53. Permeability	μ	$MLT^{-2}I^{-2}$	H/m, $\frac{Wb}{A{\cdot}m}$
54. Permittivity	ε	$M^{-1}L^{-3}T^4I^2$	F/m, $\frac{C^2}{N{\cdot}m^2}$
55. Magnetic dipole moment	μ	L^2I	$A{\cdot}m^2$
56. Magnetic field strength	H	$L^{-1}I$	A/m
57. Magnetic flux	Φ_B	$ML^2T^{-2}I^{-1}$	weber (Wb)
58. Magnetic induction	B	$MT^{-2}I^{-1}$	Wb/m^2, tesla (T)
59. Magnetization	M	$L^{-1}I$	A/m
60. Pole strength	m	LI	Am
61. Inductance	L	$ML^2T^{-2}I^{-2}$	henry (H)

Published By: NEL., Dantali
Printed By : NEL., Silvassa
CTP
2653
8-12-21